A PROPOSAL FOR LOVE

Physical, Mental, Emotional and Spiritual Health

Ethel Erickson Radmer

Titles also by Ethel Erickson Radmer

Now is Enough/Nu är det Nog: A Trip to Sweden with Three of My Grandsons

Archetype to Zest: 26 Essays for the Curious

Knowing Sarah: Lost Arts, Health Practices and Moral Guideposts

Walking the Rails: My Childhood in Whitehall

My Odyssey with Two Uncommon Boys: A Trip to the Western States

Conversations with Carl: My Journey Through Grief

The Cheshire Cat Syndrome: My Adventures with Arthritis

For Carl Radmer

My loving husband of 39 years until your death in 1997. You knew how important the study and practice of health and wellbeing was to me and you lived with the fascination I've always had with the workings of the Universe. Now that the long-ago envisaged book is written, I feel your spirit sharing my happiness. Our love was, is and always will fill our beings as part of the all-encompassing ONE.

I love you dear Carl.

CONTENTS

Chapter 1

LOVE HEALS

I've just finished reading Pia de Jong's book, *'Saving Charlotte: A MOTHER AND THE POWER OF INTUITION.'* Pia's daughter was born with congenital myeloid leukemia, 'a very dangerous form of leukemia,' as her medical professionals described it. It kills and it does it soon with very few exceptions. The chemotherapy treatment for someone so young can likely kill too. So what is a mother to do?

Pia followed her instincts, refused the treatments, and told her doctor, "No, we want to go home." And carrying her newborn, she and her husband left the hospital to nest in their house on the Herengracht canal in Amsterdam. What she chose to be and do was to be with this child every moment and to love her in all that they did, along with her supportive family of two small boys and her husband. And, as her oncologist said, "let her do it her way." Well, Charlotte slowly came back, she was alive. And then she thrived! What a testament to the power of love. Love infused her and her body responded, finding wherever and whatever the weaknesses were in her small fragility and getting all parts, miraculously, back in balance.

And I have just heard in person, Serena Dyer, daughter of Dr. Wayne and Marcelene Dyer, tell a large group of us about her infancy. She cried incessantly and there seemed no way to calm her. Her mother decided to wear her in a sling around the clock, being next to the heart of her mom and feeling the love and connection, to ease her tension. It worked. She's a beautiful, loving mother, herself, today.

And there is baby Raun, the *Son-Rise*, 1979 TV movie, child, who lived in his own world, out of touch with the people around him. His parents, Samaria and Bears Kaufman, through all their waking hours, gave him steady, enthusiastic, loving attention and acceptance. By age three he started emerging from his cocoon, smiled and said I love you to his parents and grew to become a marvelous Option Institute (center for autism treatment and for personal growth & happiness) teacher, giving love in a steady stream to adults and children alike.

And there are stories to tell later of adults who overcame intractable illnesses after they immersed themselves in love.

That brings me to the premise of this book: LOVE HEALS. Plain and simple, but profound.

Sir Isaac Newton, born in the 17th Century in England, who formulated several physical laws and is one of the most influential scientists of all time, said this, "Truth is ever to be found in the simplicity, and not in the multiplicity and confusion of things."

So now, I'll step it up a little from the simple premise LOVE HEALS to the continuing premise: LOVE IS THE PREEMINENT HEALER. Surpassing all others. If love isn't present, any healing potions or corrections, for what ails you, can't be as effective. Having no love in your being has to be oppressive down to each individual cell. So you've got to have love.

And another step further I offer a more time-inclusive premise: LOVE WAS THERE WHEN THERE WAS NOTHING AND LOVE IS THE BEGINNING OF EVERYTHING. That is huge and it is still simple.

Expanding fully now to: LOVE CREATED THE WHOLE COSMOS: EVERYTHING THAT WE KNOW AND DON'T KNOW.

That's outrageous, you say. Yes, I know. My LOVE hypotheses cover a lot of territory. But, in understanding love, we need to know where it is coming from. It is one thing to say "LOVE HEALS" and another to extend that love in answer to the BIG question: "How did all that we 'see' come about?" The answer, I say, is that Love made it happen. And, I agree with the skeptics or naysayers that it may be presumptuous for me to say something that I cannot prove scientifically. But I'm dealing with the unknowable. You can't prove the unknowable.

At the top of the 'unknowable' on the physical plane is the event horizon. The event horizon is the point, the circle, the globe, multidimensional, that you can envision in your mind's eye, encircling us in the cosmos that we cannot see beyond. The diameter of the 'observable universe' sphere is calculated to be between 84 and 93 billion light years across. We can imagine what is beyond, as being 'more of the same' of what we can 'see,' OR different in every way, with different physical laws, with many dimensions beyond our picturing, and with energies and fields and vibrations we haven't even calculated.

Having laid out my four postulates for love, a proposal in total for the vast overview of love, let's return to our infinitesimal part of the cosmos, terra firma, and to our bodies and stay basked in the beauty of LOVE HEALS and save examining in more depth the other LOVE postulates for later or another book. I spelled it out now to the endless reach of the cosmos because I want you to have the big picture and to know where I am coming from in my thinking and writing. Now, the important thing we face is what to do about our health.

LOVE HEALS. How amazing is that? And it's believable.

I have a story to tell from my years in San Francisco of a sick adolescent boy. I don't remember and can't find to remind me of the details of this young man, but I will say what I can recall from my learning about him in a medical environment. He was barely a teen when he developed a cancer that would probably kill him. He went through all the protocol rounds of chemo and radiation and it was not containing the cancer growth. His father, a medical specialist, and he the son had the idea of enlisting the entire medical community where the father worked and the son was treated, to support the boy in an active way. The large group met in a lecture hall and talked and demonstrated their love for this young man whom they really loved. They showered him with love. He saw it and felt it and could imagine a change for the good in his body. They kept up sending their love to him throughout their days. And like a miracle, the cancer retreated and could not be found. But eventually it did return and they demonstrably loved him again in a public setting. And again he seemed well and free of cancer. The love was still there to remind him. But over time the cancer won out and he died. The message for me was profound. Love healed. The body changed in whatever ways it knew it could to come into balance again. And again. And then, it seemed to be his time and the body gave out.

I know personally several adults, and there are probably many more I don't know or haven't heard about, who had fatal diseases and then had an NDE or near death experience. An NDE means they lost all their vital signs, had an experience of another world and then came back to earthly life. The remarkable thing is that they came back with no signs of their fatal illnesses. How is that possible? One of the features of an NDE is that the 1000s of cases, recorded by researchers, almost universally speak of being met on the 'other side' by 'souls' in an immersion of LOVE far, far beyond anything they have ever experienced on earth.

This tells me, as in the second postulate, LOVE IS THE PREEMINENT HEALER, that love is the 'something' that supersedes and enhances our healing beyond all of the physical adjustments and modalities we've uncovered to heal our bodies, psyches, minds and spirits.

As a long ago working occupational therapist and as an author, I have been filling files for decades with many hundreds of discoveries of what might or can cure us of our ills. And I have thought of eventually sharing all that with readers, to fill a book or more. But, over time, I've come to realize that LOVE trumps them all. If we don't have love, it's unlikely that good recovery and full health are going to happen.

Let's take infants' 'failure to thrive syndrome.' Babies, particularly from orphanages of the past, who were not touched or shown love and attention and were basically just fed and had their diaper's changed, grew slowly and stunted in mind, body and emotions, and were likely to die. They were deprived of physical contact and human touch with a loving presence. There was no love to sustain them. I heard of such stories when I was growing up in Wisconsin in the 1940s and 1950s and I felt fortunate to be in a family filled with love and caring. Present day 'failure to thrive' is attributed by medical professionals primarily to physical and nutritional causes and to abuse or neglect. And what is neglect? In a nutshell and in the broad scope it is a lack of love.

Love could have in those past days and can now today make their bodies stronger, their emotional state less flat or anxious or sad, and their minds sharper and clearer. Love nourishes all three of those bodies, and not least, our fourth body as spirit. All four bodies make up who we are and they all can use our attention.

I saved the best for last in that list to describe more fully, Spirit. Spirit comes with no hitches and no hang-ups. It is pure vibration of 'being' at a high level beyond most of our functioning on this earth. We can't measure it because it doesn't seem to have any physical qualities that our five physical senses can detect. Do you question if spirit exists? Virtually all religions on our planet believe in spirit or soul. But you don't have to be religious to know that we all have spirit. If you monitor your mind state and feel the LOVE inside your being and coming from others, how can you deny spirit in the course of your day or in your feeling the higher levels of energy that vibrate in meditation and contemplation?

What about the spirit you manifest when you run in the Olympics, pulling out all the stops to do your maximum best physically? It isn't just physical with the body at peak strength and operating with flawless coordination and unimpeded endurance, or just mental to know your task with a mind-set of doing your best, or an emotional state that does not sap but gives energy to the challenge at hand. All of those optimal actions contribute enormously to top performance. But, there seems to be something beyond your action and the neural pathways of thought and feelings that you conjure up to bring out the best in yourself. Those

Olympian champions radiate their spirit. And we speak of spirit like we know it. Their spirit carried them to the top. Spirit gave them the courage to break through any barriers. Spirit sustained them as they expended all their physical, mental and emotional energies on reaching their goal. Chris Brasher who won a gold medal in steeplechase at the 1956 Olympics said, "There is something in the Olympics, indefinable, springing from the soul that must be preserved." And Wilma Rudolph, an African-American sprinter, who had polio when she was young and told by her doctors she would never walk again, became a three time Olympic champion in 1960. To the testimony of 'spirit' she said, "Never underestimate the power of dreams and the influence of the human spirit." Spirit is part of the mix. And love permeates everything.

And here's a big wondering: What about consciousness? How does consciousness fit into this love? And, was it by chance or synchronicity (related events that occur at the same time without apparent causal connection) to help in my and your understanding, the written message, "Sanaya Says *Mind, Body, and Ever-Present Spirit,*" comes on-line at suzannegiesemann.com, on 7.2.18, the very day I was yet again deeply pondering this subject, saying "Where awareness goes, consciousness flows."

That is the light of understanding for me. What I see working is this: The energy of Love was and is and always will be present and our awareness of that love is consciousness. Consciousness, I say, is awareness infused with the vibration of love. With love's presence filling the nothingness, before anything else manifested, and the awareness of that love showing itself as consciousness, you might call them both, love and consciousness, the co-creators of all that we know, or better yet, the ONE that created everything. That's BIG, with talking eternity, but SIMPLE to explain the makings of the Cosmos. Consciousness is not alone. It is power-housed by love. Love started it all and was there all along and will be for all time and is free with no limiting time in our timeless spirit world without end. The love infusion is what has created everyone and everything that we know. I don't see any other lasting forces for the good that could create what we see and know and don't know in the past, present or future. That eternal force is love.

'Create out of nothing' is not a new concept or phrase. *Creatio ex nihilo* in my high school Latin studies would translate as "creation out of nothing" and, praise the powers that be, the creation is ongoing as *Creatio continua*! There are varying, past and present religious and philosophical beliefs, as well as scientific theories on this, but for me, it is a concept, not a religious or philosophical dictum. When there was 'nothing' there was nothing material to be sensed by consciousness. But, consciousness, which does not register as material, pervaded the cosmos. And the force infused in this awareness, the 'life' of it all was, is and will be LOVE.

These are exciting times. Knowing that love is bigger and more widespread (an understatement, since I see love as eternal and endless) than you ever thought, we can come back to earth and pick up again on exploring what love can do on our earthly, physical plane, and our immediate concern in this physical life, our health to keep us alive and well.

Kate Bowler, author of *Everything Happens for a Reason*, © 2018, thinking she could control the shape of her life, was diagnosed, at age 35, with stage IV colon cancer. Being at Duke University she has the latest medical treatments at the ready. But, she says sometimes she just wants a hug. Some of her best moments with people come with a hug or a hand on the arm. And, she knows there are others who suffer and often feel isolated and want to be touched. If they're ok with hugs, give them a hug she suggests.

There are benefits from hugging including helping depression, supporting the immune system and restoring our energy. Giving hugs from your own fount of love can be just as enriching as your receiving love from others. Hugging is our loving connection with other souls and it can nourish all four of our bodies: physical, mental, emotional and spiritual. I suggest that we love each other and show it to the hilt (but not disparagingly) to someone who is receptive and in need of help and healing.

If you're ill and think you don't have love, do not despair. You can find love, discover love, accept love and, in turn, make love in big doses for the receptive and for your own big heart full of love within you. Create your very own nest of love. Love yourself and give thoughts of love to the strangers out there and to whoever appears in your life. BE THE LOVE YOU DESIRE.

There are disappointments in anyone's life and no dearth of ups and downs. The challenge is to learn from and to 'be love' in every situation. There is hidden wisdom in feeling sadness that can prompt you to accept it, take a lesson from it and be on your way to further growth and understanding. And know that the highest vibration of our existence is love. The greatest degree of inner tranquility comes from the development of love and compassion. There is no judgement in love.

In Mark 12:31 KJV Jesus told the scribes near Jerusalem, "Thou shalt love thy neighbor as thyself." Consider your neighbor and yourself as one in spirit and in the presence of love. Love transcends physical death and joins up with the 'oneness' of consciousness that created all we know and don't know. You can be just as OK with the 'don't know' as you are with the 'know.' Life affords a continuous chance to appreciate an endless array of happenings in your moments. Be love for anything that comes your way.

Chapter 2

MORE LOVE

How we experience love on this earth is as a very strong emotion and sensation. Love makes us feel good. It affects our body with aliveness, palpitations, excitement manifested as a heightened pulsing throughout our systems, increased awareness, glowing given and received and distressing emotions put to rest. Take that description to a near-death experience and love explodes with shuddering vibrations of the sensory networks. A person's spirit, floating apart from the body in an NDE, is immersed in the glow of love of the highest order, a most dense connection and sustaining warmth beyond belief. "Love is felt a trillion times more than what we feel in our physical state," I've heard at least one NDEer say. And another has described the pure love as a powerful feeling projected from the spirit world, with complete acceptance of their being, no matter what they have done in this life.

That kind of love seems to me, like a set-up for a complete body make-over. That would make sense for what happens with many, temporarily on 'the other side' in an NDE or to earthbound people immersed in love, where there are no more signs of a fatal illness which had previously wracked the body. Even the toughest diseases to challenge us, without known cures, that we limp along with palliative measures and desperate kills (as in chemotherapy that may kill the cancerous cells but kill our own cells and sometimes kill our whole organism in the process) have disappeared with the incredible, high-decibel, vibrating infusion of love in the expanded world of spirit that NDEers may spend moments, minutes or a week of coma in. And that love can take over on the physical plane too, with no NDE, but with a deluge of love from all earthly directions and dimensions. It can happen if you're open to it and believe in it. FEEL THE LOVE!

The source of this pure love seems to me to be spirit in the biggest and most inclusive state of 'oneness' possible. And we're into terminology that religions and belief systems are built on: God, a Supreme Being, Allah, Jehovah, creator, Supreme Being and universal consciousness or conceptual force. For my own speaking and dialogue I prefer referring to 'the powers that be' or the full consciousness of the cosmos, which are less likely to come with a set of dogmas and doctrines. But, I think that all religions and belief systems aspire to our trying to reach, by whatever means, the highest development of the spirit or soul. I concur with that.

Whether or not you believe in a god, a divine source, the creator or a higher power, you are a spiritual being. If you or I resist using the term 'God' because of the religious implications, how about calling this higher level of being your higher self or the Beyond or the Mystery?

Or call God, as Carlos Castaneda, author of 14 books, calls it "an unmeasurable, indescribable force which sorcerers call intent and absolutely everything that exists in the entire cosmos is attached to intent by a connecting link."

By that thinking we are a part of everything that exists in the cosmos and are linked to that force called intent. And it means that we must have access to a storehouse of knowledge and wisdom if only we could raise our consciousness and awareness to as high a level as we can achieve. That's where the spiritual comes in. Low level griping and pining doesn't cut it for making that connection to a higher place. The spiritual aspect of our selves is at a high level of existence. And there are traits and behaviors that go along with it.

Goodness and kindness are high values, ensconced in love, and they fill the spirit with a glow, as my mother Sarah radiated from every part of her being. People knew it, could feel it, could count on it and felt better because Sarah was always there with such pure love, modest with no grandstanding and never wavering. With love you feel part of the whole. Or, as out of Sarah's well-worn KJV Bible, she would have quoted I John 4:8: He that loveth not knoweth not God; for God is love.

How we express that love is what comes naturally from your heart. You can show that love in many ways as your spirit moves you to convey it. My mother made known her love in good deeds and being available with her sincere caring and compassion. She showed it and you can too in your radiance and glow.

What about the love you feel for someone near and dear to you, beyond the emotional feelings, don't you think there is a transcendent state of bliss that brings all your feelings and thoughts and physical reactions together? We call that 'Spirit'! To all you dear spirits in the Cosmos!

I agree with the Buddhists who say that our spirit in energy form has no beginning and no end, just like the universe, and I would add, the whole cosmos and love itself.

So, our spirit bodies, filled with boundless, endless love, nourish the urges for health of our physical, mental and emotional bodies. With that unlimited love filling our spirit we can flourish, grow and glow like the blooming *Goldflower* on the tundra at the top of Mount Evans in

Colorado, our family home on a ranch for the two summers of 1965 and 1966, while Carl was hunting for quarks coming from outer space with a team of scientists. Talk about love! The big flower disk, like a sunflower, sits on top of a sturdy stem, tight up and low to the ground to stay warmer on the chilly mountaintop, and filling the space like a hundred suns! (caution to hikers to not trample the mountain mats of gold that take up to 30 years to grow!). What glory we lived midst the beauty to remind my husband, our three barely school age children and me what it is to be up at the top at 14,130 feet with the heavens above and surrounded by the golden sparkle and flare of life and light. Our spirits were raised to light-headed levels and all was sublime. If there was anything unbeknownst to be healed, the ills dissipated in a flash of glowing love surrounding us and filling our hearts – at the top of the mountain!

LOVE IS THE PREEMINENT HEALER! That is my preeminent proposal!

I back up the validity of my theorems, surprisingly, partly with the fact that there is NO scientific evidence for love being the creator of everything including the beginning of the universe and the Cosmos, and with the fact that there is little rigorous scientific evidence for LOVE healing all our physical aspects: the body, mind, emotions, and our transcendent spirit, though intuitively we know it's so. For one thing, scientific study doesn't generally take on the questions that there seem no answers to – was there a beginning and if not is there infinity and what was there in the interim of the cycle of physical manifestations? How can an ephemeral thing like 'love' be measured to do anything, much less 'heal' us? Love being hard to study scientifically means there is a gap to be filled with either continued unknowing or with speculations unfounded – that is, not substantiated with data. So 'no evidence' gives me space to come up with my own theorems that I have pondered and that make sense to me, with some anecdotal support in people's lived experiences, to fill the gap. There's a vacuum here. And I'm glad to cram it chock-full of love.

I say that what was there all along was the energetic vibration of love in a field that continually creates an endless stream of universes. The most basic intention, the impetus, the impulse and the urge of this creation of the universes is LOVE. Love is at the top and transcendent from our earthly home to a love-filled cosmos.

That answers the big questions in life more adequately for me than the dearth of scientific explanation that might always be a dearth, of the mystery of being. With love as cause, my life is a trajectory of beauty, discovery, fun and bliss.

And I have the Serbian-American inventor, engineer, and physicist, Nikola Tesla's supportive quote, "If you want to find the secrets of the universe, think in terms of energy, frequency and vibration." He also thought that in order to have peace and harmony we need to work together, not with ego, but in love.

To my partners on this high trajectory of our lives, I say, "Let's bring MORE LOVE into the world!" Our spirits could use the boost to as high a frequency as we can get.

And what makes love be the PREEMINENT healer? I believe that love can heal anything and everyone! Yes! Let the naysayers scoff. It's good to be skeptical, but if it closes the door on love, where is the hope and goodwill and kindness that we thrive on? Being fully immersed in love supersedes and makes possible any and all of the 'healing arts' to work effectively. Love is at the front and in the center. It pervades and surpasses all limits. There is no potion or emotion that can or has the possibility to heal ALL illnesses and diseases, but love. Our medical specialists and energetic healers can certainly help us heal and selectively cure. But it takes love right from the get-go to set the stage, infuse the bodies, support all actions, comfort when fear creeps in, make us know and feel for certain that we are not alone and to know we are part of the ONE. With that connection, we have a direct line to a broader awareness which is love by any measure.

Love is transcendent, gaining its power from the ONE, exceeding the accomplishments of our earthly modalities. And it is preventative, though we might not know it. But, if good health radiates from your body, mind, emotions and spirit, you are being what you want to be and are in the glow of well-being with thankfulness, you can know that our preeminent healer must be at work. It is love.

Chapter 3
LONG AGO and FAR AWAY

Long ago and far away there was nothing. Neither stars nor suns. No planets. No Jupiter's or Earth's to rotate a raging sun. No fields we could measure between those non-existent bodies, no pulsing with energetic particles, no photon waves of light. Nothing.

But … not nothing! Unseen but filling the space was the awareness of LOVE. Awareness is consciousness and it was always present and was and is ONE with LOVE. Love is the energy that filled the space of nothingness. The consciousness of love that created a field of love when there was 'nothing' set off the explosion we call The Big Bang. Remember that Science does not know what was there before the Big Bang; they only say there was 'nothing' because they do not know.

In no time at all, suddenly accelerating far, far beyond Einstein's speed limit of light, energy exploded with gusts of heat, flashes of light, waves of matter forming and scattering like a sling shot at unimaginable speed in a 360 degree, three-dimensional (or is it 4 or 5 or 25 more?!) arc, and then cooled and coalesced to form bodies, solar systems, galaxies, universes. And, where the conditions of heat, light and elements were favorable, cells, organs and organisms were created and baptized with life – and love.

And to deal with a sticky subject right away, where does the dark side of the coin or the 'not love' in the yin/yang symbol of opposites fit in? If there was love back then, as I'm saying, and we know we have love now coming from everywhere, what about violence, seeming the opposite of loving events, where did that come from? Love is manifested in so many beautiful ways we cannot deny it. But violence isn't so pleasant for humanity to face up to.

Here's my answer: Violence exists because we have free will, my companion free-thinkers! Love-filled consciousness created us with free will and a part of conscious love with free will is that there is a whole range of actions and behavior that are possible on the spectrum, including those that can possibly destroy, kill and maim. If there was not a kaleidoscope of tints and tones, we would not have choice and we would be one-dimensional. The choices of love or something less than love gives scope and meaning to the choices we do make. We are not robots - where's the fun, intrigue and freedom in that? And where is the learning in our earth school as well as in the spirit world? It is in ignorance that we might choose a lower level of action and the next time we do something more life-sustaining, growing in our manifesting goodness. We learn from that and find that we can choose love. Every person on this earth is unique with a wide range of differences that opens the door on bad (as perceived or not by the experiencer as bad or good or neutral) things happening. We know that nature is full of violence and is beautiful at the same time. But it's harder to look at the human realm and dismiss violent acts. We are civilized after all.

The biggest violent act we calculate was the Big Bang that took placed 14 billion years ago and the expanding is still going on. After unknown billions of years more it will collapse on itself to a point, a nothing singularity, and then reemerge to expand again and to be repeated and repeated in the endless, infinite cycle of expansion and contraction of the universes that I think is the inevitable, ongoing drama of histrionic theater. This biggest bang ever was a nanosecond explosive eruption of fire, heat, particles and chunks hurtling into the deep reaches of space, colliding, hitting, smashing, rounding all their rough edges to make spheres that are, over time, attracting, repelling, cooling and settling into round or elliptical orbits around a turbulent sun. Creation was and is taking place, as we speak, and it's a fierce and wondrous thing.

Violence IS. We can raise our consciousness and see that we can learn and evolve from any violence that we might be witness to or part of and that disturbs us. And we can change our view that a violent act is necessarily bad – as in one animal kills another for food in the cycle of nature and in our knowing that what seems chaotic in nature has order beneath it. Our universe gives us plenty of opportunity to learn lessons and evolve in spirit and some people view that 'school of hard knocks' as my dad would say, as where we grow and find our purpose on this earth. I don't see it so much as our purpose but as 'rising above the fray is the best thing to do.' It is in the midst of turmoil that the most beautiful happening can transpire! If you look for it!

And the same goes for fear and hate. Rise above it! They seem the opposite of love. They are constricting emotions that pull us back and weigh us down. Whereas, the love we know expands and flows through all things with ease and awareness. Fear and hate compress, destroy and dissolve. Love radiates and creates. It is all part of the yin and yang of existence and energy. We might work our way out of fear and hate and then evolve and emerge like a butterfly with the chrysalis transforming from its home in a cocoon to a full adult butterfly with wings to fly with ease to take it anywhere. Free and filled with love. As First John 4:18 says: There is no fear in love.

In an NDE you are not judged for acts that are anything less than love. You, in seeing the range of possibilities and choices, can totally love and it is such an edifying way of being. Hate, revenge and anger are on the lower end of one's chart of development. It's such a nice contrast to be high on the curve of love.

And this is big. Anything we perceive as negative is an opportunity to give and receive love. The more love we send to humanity and nature and to the upper reach of our higher source, the more everything and everyone benefits and our four bodies are healthier for the love showers. Emotions are on a high. Mind is computing and analyzing like clock-work. Body is in ship-shape to do whatever you ask of it. Our spirits are elevated and always filled with the power of love.

As Michel LeGrand wrote the music and Norman Gimbel the English words for *Watch What Happens*, one of my favorite songs to play on the piano and to sing,

> *Let someone with a deep love to give*
> *Give that deep love to you*
> *And what magic you'll see.*

Love's power to heal others and ourselves is like magic. Love transforms the body when we flip a switch to receive and to give love.

To further inspire, here is a married couple with a story that was told in news outlets around the globe and with a TV appearance on *Today* in 2018, who were losing their newborn, two pound, premature son (twin to a newborn, 2 pound, premature but healthy girl). His heartbeat was nearly gone and he stopped breathing, with the doctor seeing he would die in moments. To cherish their tiny son, Kate and David, with his shirt off, unwrapped and lovingly cuddled their boy to give him warmth and love contact against their bare skin and talked to him, saying how hard they had tried to have him and enticing him to stay with a twin sister to love. And the miraculous happened. Their son, Jamie, gasped and he started to breath. Then he opened his eyes and reached for his father's finger. Their almost-lost boy had made it and they felt like the luckiest people in the world. The twins learned this story when they were eight years old. Here is a miracle of love. Jamie's body and spirit were swathed in love and he responded with a finger connection. All he wanted was love.

I think, in all of us, there is an inner urge, an instant resolve to sustain our vitality. If there is an emergency challenging our life force then our push to stay alive goes into action. Why? Because we feel the love! We're made of love and born with a base of love to launch our human existence and when we feel the love connection to those souls who love us, we are implored to overcome any hurdle and to be a life-love force.

And, with a sign-off by the Beatles and a sign-on to life:

"All you need is love
all you need is love.
All you need is love, love,
love is all you need."

Chapter 4

PHYSICAL, MENTAL and EMOTIONAL CHALLENGES

Now, dig in your heels, fasten your seatbelts co-inhabitants of this spinning ball of earth. You are in for an intense ride. We have dealt with the all-encompassing cosmic view, asking and answering the biggest questions in the minds of the curious, and now we can deaccelerate from the vastness of nothing and everything, and return to our earthly humanity, housed in the human body, taking in and comprehending the physical and spiritual state of things, machinations, intentions, limitations, capabilities, and emotional states, warts and all, that are in all of us, but that are still part of and connected with the vast field of energy that I call love. There's some heavy lifting here to 'get' the complexity of our working 'selves,' so let's take the jump onto the roller-coaster of life.

On this material/physical plane we have a physical body to contain our spirit. Being in a physical state means that our bodies, minds and emotions are vulnerable to a host of physical impacts, invasions, imperfections, imbalances, and ignorance (we have limits, often self-imposed, on how much knowledge we can retain). What most of us and maybe all would want is that all parts of our being would function optimally, without pain or distress or an early death. Granted, whatever ailments we have can be a learning device for our reaching a higher level of spirit awareness. But life is easier if we can manage to avoid the things that are not good for our body, mind and emotional state and do what is better to reach a state of ease, comfort, and vibrant health.

And to clarify and differentiate, our emotional health encompasses the feelings we have about things. Generally, feelings can be comfortable or uncomfortable, exciting or boring, pleasant or unpleasant, and uplifting or upsetting, with a range in-between extreme. Some of those feel good or not feel good feelings can be described as affection, grief, empathy, hate, elation, joy, rage, peaceful, remorse, shame, satisfied, and love. It's a potpourri of ups and downs in our emotional state. Balance for our wellbeing is vital. Freedom from all upsetting emotions is the ideal but hard to attain since our humanity is challenged daily. But, if those emotions that gnaw at and disturb our equilibrium are balanced with love, our health can become radiant. And, believe it or not, I think total, complete, non-ending love is really possible and would make for a poised steadiness and a solid footing which is expansive enough to carry you past any outside blows or inside alarms.

Our mind needs health too. Mind is busy thinking thoughts about things, sometimes with clarity and easy access to knowledge and sometimes muddled and frantic. The mind is practiced at doing mental processing in learning and in understanding abstract concepts but it can easily be disturbed. It judges, criticizes, dwells on disasters and gets stuck on ruminations. We need to give it a rest and get to a peaceful state, a state of mind where there is no thing and nothing is everything.

To realize how we might get to our best state of radiant health, let's review what we already have learned and know about our bodies and add new knowledge we've acquired to our picture of what can ail us, giving examples, and here and there, suggestions of what we have done and can do about it on our earthly plain.

My overarching belief is that the more we know and better understand the workings and nuances of our bodies and diseases and the more we see the makings, the what and the how of our body functions and its shortcomings, the better we can realize intuitively what the physical body, mind, emotions and spirit are saying and the more likely we can find ways to change, accommodate, circumvent, overcome, dissolve and finally repose the turbulence to a state of healing and recovery from all that ails us. You have the intelligence and the radar to sense what is best for you and to know when and how to intervene and stay in the prime of health and well-being. And then, in this tranquil, untroubled state of wellness for all four of our bodies, feel the peace and glow and let our consciousness rise as cream rises to the top, and then feel the joy of knowing that in a state of higher awareness of being, we have and always have had love. As in my theorem LOVE IS THE PREEMINENT HEALER.

With love as our base and our guide, let's look over the landscape of health and disease and dive into the details.

There are 1000s of medically defined, mental, emotional and physical diseases (cancer as one example), illnesses (asthma), disorders (anxiety and panic disorders), deformities (cleft palate), deficiencies (Vitamin D deficiency in rickets), conditions (gastroesophageal reflux disease – acid in stomach backs up into esophagus), malfunctions (Addison's disease -- adrenal hypofunction with low cortisol), syndromes (Cushing's syndrome – hormonal disorder with a steady stream of excess cortisol in the blood from too much cortisol being produced in adrenal glands or too much cortisol in medications), and any causes of ill health which may pervade and situate in many if not most humans and animals

(animals have a lot of similar conditions and diseases to we humans). And there are bodily injuries and damage of all sorts to challenge any idea of 'normal function.' We all know, perhaps intimately, many labels in this lexicon of ill health.

Then, there are groupings of these variants from health I've given above, which can be put into more categories, such as neurological disorders (ALS), infections (fungal, bacterial, unknown agents), cardiovascular malfunctions (heart valve not working), metabolic hypo and hyper function (diabetes—not enough insulin), and many more categories and listing within groups. All are deviations from a state of health.

MS or multiple sclerosis is in the category of neurological disorders as well as auto immune disorders (where the body attacks its own cells) and possibly in a third category -a genetically determined disorder of metabolically dependent neurodegeneration (JAMA Neurology October 2004), a mouthful (!) but essentially it means that any MS relapses are caused by metabolic changes. I have three women friends with multiple sclerosis who are doing well, even over many years, with mild exacerbations and good recovery in times of remission, and are getting around and seeing pretty normally.). Another friend with MS recently died after needing a wheel chair early on, with progression to computer aided moving and communicating. MS is a neurological disorder that kills off, in a spotty fashion and with varying degrees of aggressiveness, the myelin sheath of, potentially, most any nerve in the body. That leads to spotty transmission of nerve signals. Some of the possible impairments include partial blindness, loss of muscle control, numbness, and apathy – yes, it can affect the brain too, as in Parkinson's disease with depression. Remissions and exacerbations are a feature of MS so one might have long stretches of recovering some use of body parts and then have an exacerbation with more myelin damage. The medics have a toolbox of pharmaceuticals that delay exacerbations, lessen inflammation and ease pain and of therapies to keep joints moving and muscles working. But there is no cure.

The Persian poet, Rumi, living in the 13th century, wrote "The cure for pain is in the pain." Perhaps, if we stretched our imagination, we could sit in the middle of that pain and let love take over like a golden light shining into every hurting body part or pained emotional space. Feel the love and be grateful for the repose. And keep it up again and again to help establish a new route through the neural networks messaging calm and to solidify a pattern of repeated love impulses to cancel out the discomfort, now in the past.

Can LOVE overcome these maladies and even prevent them in the first place? Love is a powerful and creative force and all things are possible. Jesus walked on water in Matthew 14:22-33 - was it metaphoric? The laws of science say you cannot walk on water. But, belief is possible if you just believe. I believe that love could make a positive difference to prevent or to handle any challenge one faces and that the positive, upbeat force of love can ward off negative emotional weights and penetrate all the body's cells to do their best at staying alive and be decidedly functional. That helps and at the least, does not hinder.

Besides MS, the auto-immune category of disease contains virtually all neurological disorders: myasthenia gravis (neuromuscular disease of skeletal muscle weakness), Guillain-Barre syndrome (immune system damages peripheral nervous system causing muscle weakness), Huntington's chorea (an inherited disorder that kills brain cells), and muscular dystrophy (genetic disorder causing progressive weakness and loss of muscle mass). Also included for autoimmunity are lupus, rheumatoid arthritis, celiac disease, Addison's disease, many metabolic malfunctions like diabetes, and the list goes on for what could be auto-immune, including well over 100 diseases, and counting. Somehow the body mistakes its own tissue for a foreign agent to get rid of and that can create havoc and eventually death. All autoimmune disorders give an immune response to systemic inflammation that leads your body to attack itself.   In modern medicine, pharmaceuticals are used to manage symptoms and research focuses on toxicity of mutant proteins, the role of different blood cells, and anything else that might be contributing to the disease, even before the illness shows, and to develop newer drugs to counteract symptoms and reduce systemic inflammation and ideally to figure out why any of these neurological diseases occur.

In diabetes the immune system attacks and destroys insulin-producing cells in the pancreas. In rheumatoid arthritis the immune system attacks and destroys the lining of your joints that leads to inflammation that can affect your entire body. Addison's disease, that my husband had, as did President John F. Kennedy, attacks the adrenal glands that produce cortisol and aldosterone. Vasculitis, as an immune disorder, attacks and narrows the arteries and veins that restrict blood flow. And the list goes on.

Psychosis takes up prominent space in the Mental and Behavioral Disorders category. Approximately 1 percent of the population suffers from a psychotic disorder, which can include several forms of schizophrenia. Psychosis is a syndrome of hallucinations, delusions and confusion of thought.

Psychosis presents a challenge to our wondering why it happened and what to do about it. People who have one or more psychotic episodes are disconnecting from the reality of our world, but maybe for just some of the time. Professionals can give psychoanalytic and psychological support to the person vulnerable to psychotic episodes, particularly, to help them deal with an assortment of disorienting and disturbing delusions and hallucinations, such as believing things that are not true, seeing or hearing things that are not there, thinking and speaking that is jumbled and confused. We give them antipsychotic drugs such as Haldol or Thorazine, among many offered, very possibly for a lifetime, to tame the symptoms and prevent the symptoms from returning. These drugs work on chemicals such as dopamine and serotonin already in the brain, to try to achieve a chemical balance that does not set off more psychotic behavior. But, the reality is that we do not know cause or cure. Just like with schizophrenic thinking, the reality for us is askew – we can't figure out the why, wherefore, or what to do about it.

This person might be much loved with caring family support and be very loving themselves or maybe not, or depressed or even happy. Whatever the state of love or lack of it in a person suffering, your beaming golden rays of love, moving in all directions, can only be for the good. Give love in spite of, because of, in lieu of, in order to be an anchor for the person having trouble reading reality. Your loving self keeps their connection to you and our world alive and maybe, with your unequivocal, non-stop loving embrace, there can grow a more solid footing with our shared reality. Support, caring, embracing, and understanding are vital for the life of that person in the midst of mental turmoil. Be a solid rock for them to spot in their most fearful moment, to reach for and find comfort in the love. At the same time, you as a loving supporter need to monitor your own state of being, knowing when you should retreat and nourish yourself and give your own body and spirit big doses of love.

Another impactful grouping within the category of Mental and Behavioral Disorders is major depression, one of the most common mental disorders in the United States, and we're talking millions. Depression can severely limit one's ability to carry out major life activities. Over 6% of all U.S. adults (more female than male) adding up to over 16 million adults in the US, and 300 million people worldwide, according to the World Health Organization, have experienced a major depressive episode. I dare say we all know someone with major depression. There are pills to take, support groups to join, meditation practices with a group or alone in your own designated quiet space, regular exercise programs, all to help raise your spirits, literally and physiologically. Research shows that movement throughout the day works. Depression saps energy and requires herculean efforts for someone to start and keep going with the work and the action that helps. But function they do and many improve and are grateful for a good day.

Love is VITAL here. Loads of it is called for, especially to counter low self-esteem, common in a depressed mind. We're talking steady love, the kind that someone with shaky self-worth can count on, can climb out of the depths of sadness with, and hang on to for their own dear life. Again, keep checking your own state of mind, to know that you are in balance with all the elements and can overflow with that glorious love that you are made of.

A new friend, Ingrid Honkala, a marine scientist, tells her story in *A Brightly Guided Life* © 2017. She says that any resentment she has felt toward people in her life has vanished and all that remains is love. Love healed her wounds and for years she has had no depression and sickness. She sees that love comes when there is understanding and forgiveness.

I'll add that understanding another person's behavior and forgiving anyone you feel needs forgiving is best done in your own mind (avoid doing it in-person because that person might not feel they need forgiving and you may have put them in an awkward spot). The love that healed my friend is the same love that heals emotional trauma of anyone, which can then give good health to any-body and not least, to our spirit.

Now, for those without the means or intention or motivation to search out a professional for help with their issues weighing them down or even if you do see a professional now and want to add more 'please listen to me' to your getting help (I know people who do that with benefits), here is just one idea of many that might be easier to tap into and provide comfort for a needy soul. Look up *Sidewalk Talk. Sidewalk Talk*, a community listening project started by psychotherapists with Traci Ruble as Founder and Director, is a recent phenomenon that I see as giving love. I personally know several people who have been trained on line to be part of a scheduled group of listeners and at least one who has been a 'talker' on the streets of the Tenderloin in San Francisco and in 40 U.S. cities and 12 countries. Any person walking the streets and seeing the tables can sit on a chair near a trained listener and talk. Whatever they want to say they share with the listener, be it their emotional pain, their worries of self-care and disease, or their sense of isolation. The listener is fully engaged, meeting the speaker's eye, listening with compassion, and conveying warmth, with an occasional supportive comment when appropriate. And the one talking, when they are ready, can leave with a sense of connection that might be a rare experience for them. You can apply this thinking to your own everyday occurrences. Listen, if your 'spirit' moves you, to someone else's travails. There is no need for you to 'advise' and it's probably best not unless there are specific questions like 'where can I find a therapist?' Just 'be' with the person for even seconds or minutes for them to know they are not alone.

There's no data on the effects on the talkers or the listeners in *Sidewalk Talk*. But, people have anecdotally responded with "It's so great." "I'm glad to have you listen." A listener can almost see a weight lifted from shoulders of the talker and says, "And it's such a great thing."

I see this all as love. Connection. Kindness. Caring for another that might have a profound impact on another's life as well as their own. With the good reports I've heard about Sidewalk Talk from both the talker and the listener, it does seem to benefit them both. And what a good thing that is! Playing in all our heads and hearts could be Hal David's written words and Burt Bacharach music, "What the world needs now is love, sweet love. It's the only thing that there's just too little of. What the world needs now is love, sweet love, No not just for some but for everyone."

That might be what Carl Rogers, the well-known psychotherapist of the 1950s to 1980s, in my early lifetime, had in mind with his client centered listening and repeating school of psychology. His way of thinking was at a peak when I was a UW Madison student enrolled in *Abnormal Psychology.*

And then there is this to make a case for listening and connection. I've been part of a group in long-ago past years (and still existing and current) called *Speaking Circles* founded and led by a friend, Lee Glickstein in the San Francisco Bay area. The whole group of up to ten gives silent support and connection to one of those same people, each of whom has a turn up front. Many come with life-long stage fright (surveys show that people fear public speaking more than they fear death!) and all are immediately welcomed with acceptance and warmth and no judging. The key for the speaker is to 'be with' one audience member at a time, looking directly into their eyes and to feel an intimate inclusion, while the person up front is speaking spontaneously or is pausing in quiet, as their 'spirit' moves, all including the audience and speaker, feeling a part of the shared warmth, focused attention given, and heart-felt connection made that I call and felt as LOVE.

Again, that might be what Carl Rogers had in mind!

And of course, there are many well-defined psychiatric and psychological disorders, that I haven't named, that are prevalent in our population, needing our serious attention. They can use a continuing, hefty dose of love, too. And the love will come to them and out from them in precious moments to savor, like their child hugging them and showing an awareness of their sadness, an empathy that we might long for and feel is in short supply.

Dr. Bill Thomas, medical director of the Memorial Nursing home in New Berlin, NY and written about in *Being Mortal* by Atut Gawande © 2014, saw early on in his job that boredom, loneliness and helplessness pervaded the nursing home. Most residents were older, about half with disabilities & four out of five had Alzheimer's or related dementia. He decided with the help of the Board, the staff and the residents to make a radical change. Despair, that was prevalent, gave way to dogs and cats, birds, live plants (somehow accommodating those who had allergies or didn't want the closeness of animals), sharing space with individuals and floors. Children of staff came after school to hang out, a garden was planted by friends out back and everything changed. The whole place came alive! People took responsibility for the animals' care and to give attention to and love these creatures. There was reason to intermingle. In other words, new life was injected into their home and they rose to the occasion. It brought out their slumbering humanity and their love and affection started flowing among all the residents, animals, plants and kids. It transformed the space and their lives. To my mind that speaks of LOVE. What a difference love can make in the mental and emotional and physical health of anyone, even in the evening of life on this planet.

But, back to more categories to put diseases in are those with different modes of working. They include acute vs. chronic, primary vs. secondary, and local vs. systemic diseases, terms that are pretty common knowledge and self-explanatory. And from my observing point of view, I can see these 'modes of working' as a reflection of how each individual is

    A PROPOSAL FOR LOVE   Ethel Erickson Radmer

responding to an intrusion on their own health. Such as with an acute illness happening at a weak point in a person's functioning and overcoming it with reassessment of their wholeness. Or, as in a chronic settling in but not fully overcoming the challenges to reach health and then a letting go of interferences that have hung on and on, to the body, mind and psyche's great relief. And Love is at the top in any program to restore your wellness. Remember to be loved and to love – for all you're worth! And you're worth a lot. Every single one of you is loveable and loved with the warm blanket of eternal, ever-powerful, infinite Oneness of Love Consciousness embracing you.

There are organ diseases, including ones I've spoken of earlier in the text like a sick pancreas having diabetes and at the same time being in the inflammatory and sometimes infectious disease categories. The pancreas can develop pancreatitis, with pain, fever and vomiting. The heart, the most important organ of all to keep us alive, with its life sustaining pumping, has innumerable things that can go wrong. And the skin, as the largest organ in the body, can easily be seen covering our frame. The skin is capable of showing visible signs of scaling, rashes, infection and it hints, when the expert doctor picks it up, of cancerous growths.

And you can take any organ of the human body, like the spinal cord and attach a host of diseases like tumors, meningitis, polio, and spinal muscular atrophy that might fit in other categories as well, as in the groupings of infections, inflammatory and degenerative diseases.

I think that having a bigger picture of what we're dealing with in disease can help our understanding of what is happening and perhaps make us wiser to what to do about it.

We might think like Louise Hay, founder of Hay House Publishing and author of twenty books, to look for connection between the disease and what our behavior and attitude is. As in what Louise Hay says in *Heal Your Body* © 1988, listing many diseases: "The 'Problem' is 'Rheumatism.' The 'Probable Cause' is 'Feeling victimized. Lack of love. Chronic bitterness. Resentment.' The 'New Thought Pattern' is 'I create my own experiences. As I love and approve of myself and others, my experiences get better and better.' "

My own thought is that you can't do better than 'As I love and approve of myself and others, my experiences get better and better.' It's worth repeating!

Another phenomenon that might shed light on the LOVE HEALS hypothesis is this. With many illnesses there is a prodrome (early sign or warning) that might appear months or years before the disease manifests. There is the prodromal migraine aura (almost all of us have heard of or know people with this) to warn of a neural storm to come in the brain. Or there is fever, headache and no appetite, a precursor of infective disorders to come. Losing one's sense of smell is a prodrome of Parkinson's neurological weaknesses appearing. And there are dogs, extremely sensitive to smell, who smell cancer on their human companion and lick a spot as if to remove it and nudging and urging the person to give attention to this – a mole on a leg or a systemic cancer that has yet to be diagnosed. I've known a few people with this experience, including a veterinarian who has seen it several times with pet keepers and their animals that he treats in his practice. Is it inevitable that early signs lead to a full-blown disease? I don't think so. We can take those hints and clues as a chance to redress our ways and embrace a healthier life that benefits all our bodies. With the gift of signs, we have opportunity to forestall, maybe prevent, and make changes in our lives. If our relationship with others is in disarray it could be an opportunity to reassess our own behavior, forgive and offer love, just love to make amends and fill the spaces. At the least you will feel better.

How can we use this information on diseases? What more can we make of this?

There is no cure for many diseases and illnesses (we have a long ways to go!), but medicine is steadily on the hunt for drugs that depress the disease's progress, ameliorate symptoms and relieve discomfort. That goes for many neurological disorders, mental and behavioral disorders, heart disease (surgery might correct malfunction), strep throat (antibiotic will stop the infectious process) and in autoimmune disorders, such as Sjorgren's syndrome where mucous membranes don't secrete enough tears and saliva, they are relieved somewhat with medications, and in infections such as AIDS where a pharmacy full of chemicals are juggled to slow the devastating progress of symptoms that might eventually kill the host. It is an infectious virus that attacks the immune system in AIDS and is an example of many illnesses that cross 'category' and 'grouping' lines to present special challenges in figuring out cause and cure, if possible, and ways to slow the progression of infection and contagion. A dose of love can help counter the fear that is prevalent with a scary diagnosis. Fear has been shown in studies to interfere with a good recovery. Love supports it. And love might do a lot more in preventing sickness in the first place, as well as in getting well.

Dealing with all the things that make us sick has a history of finding things that make us better. The past and the present have included potions, herbs, hot packs, medicine men, exorcism, prayers, hands-on healers and poisons. It seems medieval to us but there are many poisons used in the past as well as today, including chemotherapy for overcoming serious diseases. Twenty five hundred years ago arsenic was known as a poison and began being used in treatment for cancer and syphilis. 400 years ago that same chemical element arsenic, symbol As, atomic number 33 (number revered by some religions as being of God), was used to treat leukemia. In leukemia the bone marrow produces too many immature white blood cells. Giving arsenic coincided with a lowering of the blood cell count which seemed to stop leukemia's progression in its tracks. But, too much arsenic led to sickness and death. Arsenic was also used to treat Hodgkin's lymphoma, asthma, eczema, psoriasis, and Addison's disease.

Finding chemicals, fine-tuning compounds, seeing what these substances could do and finding a balance in all treatment ingredients that has a desired effect but doesn't kill seem to be the goal. But, the 'what' - symptoms and what led up to them, the 'why' - what caused it to happen, and going backward in time, what was the most original cause? and the 'wherefore' -where did it come from, continue to loom. I dare say most of the old ways of treating sickness are still used in some fashion, with some modification and in some cultures where wisdom of the elders passes on for centuries. Treatments now may be updated with the latest inventions and technology, seeing the results of research studies, and reading a steady stream of new books with new information. Surgeries are vastly more complex and possible than they ever were. But there are still things to learn from the past.

Today, modern medicine rules the roost for common use and credibility. The medical field has proliferated with high technology practices and products that survived rigorous research. They deserve our attention and consideration by anyone looking for help. It has much to offer and may solve or ameliorate a host of problems. Traditional medicine can usually manage well any variants from health, with some shortcomings that we all have experienced our own versions of. And there are also alternative approaches to getting well that many people, including myself, subscribe to.

Alternative medicine is a huge industry in the U. S. and around the world, but it doesn't have the research backing that mainstream medicine has, to be certain of 'what these modalities can do.' But changes have occurred in the medical culture, with doctors approving of, recommending and referring patients to many practices, like massage, acupuncture, homeopathy, energy-work, myriad dietary supplements, and light therapy. And you can add to that, developing a healthy life style with exercise including weight lifting and stretching, healthful eating, modifying stress by 'letting go' of emotional tension, and knowing the importance of 'spiritual' support as in a religious practice or an activity group of special talents and interests or a mantra of gratefulness and joy. A lot of people engaging in these practices feel better in every way. And giving and receiving love is at the top.

Health and healing are freely discussed in the public domain and in our group consciousness. What a wonderful thing. We have much to study, consider and choose from and we can read and talk about it freely with most anyone. The culture, having become so knowledgeable and open on health issues, is a significant support for our own health.

So, the poi puree is there for the taking, choices can be in the making, and I think that love enhances, supersedes, and rises above them all.

Love is the greatest gift as in 1 Corinthians 13:2,13 (NKJV) of the Bible. "And though I have the gift of prophecy, and understand all mysteries and all knowledge, and though I have all faith, so that I could remove mountains, but have not love, I am nothing." "And now abide faith, hope, love, these three; but the greatest of these is love."

Chapter 5

BIG

BALANCE

But, there's more! There are overarching and standout health issues, that we've already touched on, that can have a huge impact on our state of being, which I've chosen and see as BIG. Balance, Immunity, and Genetics are the Big Three. There certainly are others, but these three, I think loom large, with their strongly impacting all aspects of disease and our health and wellbeing. They deserve a book or more too! But I'll pare it down for easy digestion and absorption, as in our digestive tract working optimally!

Balance is key for warding off disease. Imbalance throws everything (including people around you!) into disarray. Chemicals produced and signals given in the body, if not precisely and continuously managed by your body, throw your system out of balance. If you have an emotional heap of grief for a loss, it weighs heavy until you can tip the balance scale with loving acts of kindness given and received and with joy consciously created in each precious moment of your day.

Your spirit might know more than any part of you that you are out of or in balance. Fear, disharmony and demands of ego throw you into a state of instability and noncomposure. Free flowing love will help your body restore that balance. Live in love and then negativity will bother you less. Care, compassion and kindness will fill the gap. Align the lower energy of your thinking with your awareness of the highest vibration of all and that is Love. Love, equivalence and harmony are all one.

A healer's hands bring love-filled energy to put you back in balance and at peace, even with chaos swirling around you. My yogic poses center all my bodies – emotional, mindful, physical and spiritual. A stretch one direction is balanced with a stretch in the other direction. The body consciousness knows this with every cell computing position and settings and groundings and locus and bringing it back to stasis and parity. And love is the energy that infuses every cell and soul with well-being. What can be in better balance than that?

Fear, ill will, animosity, misery, apathy, neglect, disharmony and sorrow cannot survive in a field of love. Call them the opposites of love, but love is so much grander, bigger and enveloping. Fear and its attendant draining energies cannot survive when love's presence and power is felt. Love is an endless field of energy, wiggling into and taking over any negativity, and filling up all space.

When you have a bodily injury to any body part, especially to connective tissue and joints in limbs and the spine, the body's balance is thrown off. It behooves us to reposition, realign, stabilize and nourish all injured body parts to heal well, so movement can be resumed normally.

In July 2018, two of my grown grandsons and I visited Tōdai-ji, the Great Buddha Hall, in Nara, Japan. The world's largest brass Buddha and the largest wooden Buddha, Binzuru, are both sitting high up in lotus position. My grandson, who is a resident of Japan, told me that Binzuru is a healing Buddha. You are to touch with your one hand the part of your body that needs healing and, at the same time, reach high to touch with your other hand the matching part of you that is ill or have injured, on the sitting Buddha. I had to think quickly where I wanted a healing. I had, on an earlier day, overstretched my right knee ligaments and muscles sitting in semi-lotus. I had been limping a little for a couple of days on our extensive walks. So, I touched my right knee with my left hand and at the same time with my other hand reached to touch the Buddha's right knee and I thought 'healing' and immediately forgot about it as we moved on to our next site. The next day it took me a while to realize while we were again walking, that my knee was fine with no discomfort. I was walking as I always did, in balance, with both sides operating like a machine in sync. I was healed. But what made for the healing? Time? My state of mind? The placebo effect? The powers that be channeling energy through the Buddha to me, to heal and to put my knee back in balance? I'd like to think that it was love, not far-fetched, knowing Binzuru's reputation of generously spreading high energy to all who wished to benefit from those powers. What else is a kind, compassionate act, a gift of healing force called than love? And that loving gesture matched my own font of love to create a balanced state of healing. Thank you, Binzuru!

So, balance yourself into harmony, as a musical composition written in harmony can touch your soul, and restore your energy centers to health. I've done that 1000s of times with my piano and voice and beloved French horn. Love yourself back to that familiar state of equipoise. Flow and bend to keep all parts in accord. When you have signs and symptoms of disease, instead of fear that gets you further out of balance, just give space to and a chance for the wisdom of your body to heal itself. Other bodies have done it and you can too. Being in balance is the best state to be in.

Vertigo is a sense of imbalance in our body movements, accompanied by dizziness, tinnitus and sometimes nausea. There can be many causes and many possible solutions to resolving it or at least taming it. Feeling like you're tipping can go from mild inconvenience to extreme distress that puts one to bed to avoid standing or walking. The ear with its vestibular system, as in Meniere's disease, BPPV or benign paroxysmal positional vertigo (the most common cause of vertigo), and ear infections, are one focus of vertigo. Another focus is the central nervous system, with possible viral meningitis or stroke. Both can be culprits for provoking this sense of imbalance in your head. You can search this out with medical doctors and physical and occupational therapists for diagnosis and a variety of treatments; including food triggers, dehydration, antibiotics and the Epley maneuver - a quick movement of the head to either side while lying down to reposition your inner ear calcium crystals that have become loose.

I've heard of one extreme case of vertigo (and there are hundreds more) of a woman who quit her job, walks her dog and stays put in her house. She says that family and professional support and love are essential to keep her life somewhat 'in balance.'

If close 'others' aren't available in one's life (and be aware that there are thousands out there without close or dependable ties - and please, important point - know that that doesn't make anyone bad or have to make anyone sad, that's just how it is), remember that YOU are available to yourself. Give yourself tons of love. Be as good to yourself as you can be to your four bodies which are just asking for your attention. Your physical, mental, emotional and spiritual states can rise above the trials and meet the challenges of this dizzy and hopefully temporary state of being.

You could sum this up for all health challenges by seeing and saying that you have a clear INTENTION to be well AND you know that it is POSSIBLE to be in full, vibrant health.

Homeostasis is the key word in balance. It is the tendency of our bodies to have equilibrium between interdependent elements in physiological processes. It's a work in continuous progress. The body works to maintain steady levels of temperature and other vital conditions such as the water, salt, sugar, protein, fat, calcium and oxygen in body tissues and in the blood.

Your body is a chemical factory that miraculously measures and weighs all ingredients in the precise amount that is needed to keep all our systems working in balance. There are many examples of this including the endocrine system which produces hormones for energy. All the body chemicals balance each other in exact amounts or else disease occurs, such as too little insulin in diabetes or too much cortisol that produces growth failure in a child. The metabolic system uses stores of glucose that it measures to fuel muscle contractions. The digestive system releases the digestive hormone gastrin in the stomach to secrete enzymes in the gastric glands and releases another digestive hormone secretin in the duodenum to secrete enzymes in the pancreas and liver to do their job. It's a complicated set of chemicals and actions that keeps us humming. Neurotransmitters such as serotonin are needed in exact amounts for normal brain function. Our blood needs vitamin B9 and B12, with the iron containing protein hemoglobin, to make red blood cells to carry oxygen to the body tissues and take away carbon dioxide and thus power metabolism.

These processes are all complicated and precise, one hinging on another, with measured amounts of many chemicals that influence each other to do a job to keep us functioning and alive. It is awesome to realize! And, as an aside – or maybe most important of all, you wonder is there an intelligence behind the collection of multi-level, complex, interdependent systems that we house in our body? In my limited self-conscious understanding, the total consciousness that is imbued and pulsing with the vibrating force of love and that fills every part of the universe IS creating it all. As they say about a surprise appearance, "It DID just materialize out of thin air!" But that thin air was 'nothing' but the energy of love filled consciousness – not to be measured, and creating a universe and everything in it!

In continuing to balance all physical workings our bodies need salt, but not too much and not too little. Going to the cell level, homeostasis is a balancing act. Osmosis is the movement of solvent molecules – in this case salt, through the cell's permeable membrane to the next cell that has a higher solute concentration; in the direction that equalizes the solute concentration on the two sides of the wall. There needs to be a balance of not too much and not too little salt in our cells. Salt leeches water from the cells of plants and humans and if you consume too much salt it can cause high blood pressure which can damage organs, lead to dehydration and even kill if you drank enough sea water. Too little salt can lead to cramps, coma and death. We want a balanced amount in our system and you have to find that out with your own common sense and experience and, need be, a professional's advice.

The alkaline to acidity pH levels in the body work to be in balance. Your blood pH should be slightly alkaline. Your stomach pH, around 3 on a scale of 1 to 14, is necessarily, very acidic in order to break down food. Your urine pH varies with the food you eat and it is best to have it slightly more alkaline, that is on a scale of 1 to 14, around 7 is good. Too much acid in the body fluids is called acidosis, which can disturb many body functions, including those of your kidneys and lungs. Keep checking your urine with a pH test strip from the pharmacy if you wonder. A suggestion to keep your pH level alkaline is to take a teaspoon or less of apple cider vinegar in a glass of water every morning.

A correct pH balance – slightly alkaline, in our body's billions of cells, is needed for us to function and stay alive. If your pH is off a lot of other things in the body will be off and you are vulnerable to disease. Oxygenation functions at its highest level in a slightly alkaline state. We need oxygen carried to every cell and for every body function, more than anything, to stay alive. If we didn't get oxygen in 3 minutes, as with an unconscious person not breathing or a drowning person who is rescued and given CPR, permanent brain damage begins and death can occur as soon as 4 to 6 minutes later.

These past paragraphs on balance hold just a few examples of many hundreds of chemical, hormonal, vitamin, mineral, enzyme, pH, etc. balancing going on in our bodies, continuously, probably without our awareness, to maintain good health. All our physiological systems including respiration, circulation, digestion and more are set and adjusted to keep whole-body homeostasis or equilibrium working and thus, prevent disease from setting in.

Love your body, mind, emotions and spirit enough to do good things for all your selves in their upkeep. Support health wherever it takes you, to watching and measuring your intake of liquids, minerals, enzymes and food, to challenging your balance in Chi Gong, yoga and hiking.

Then, there is this glaring issue in the culture around us, to challenge not only our physical but our emotional, mental and spiritual balance, as well. It is technology and change. How do we maintain equilibrium while having our lives continuously interwoven with computers, devices, adaptors, links, smart phones, texting, photographs, CDs, flash drives and what's next?, all acting instantly and sometimes near simultaneously, with multiple ways to 'talk' in abbreviated fashion or code, which leads often to less connecting than there would have been a couple of decades ago with much less technology, because of misses, misunderstandings, errors, misuse, mistakes, malfunctions, inattention, security measures and breakdowns. And the change! Rapid fire action, growth, innovation and the 'new' materializes every moment of the day, if we're awake to it. It's enough to break us down: body, mind, emotions and, not least, the spirit. Those bodies don't seem equipped to deal with such a radical transformation of how we now relate to others and ourselves. Change can be hard to take. But, with tech's impact on every aspect of our lives mushrooming at such a fast pace, our bodies can get exhausted with the impact. If you and I are on our own without help or attention, it can be a tough row to hoe.

Well, hang on co-occupants of this planet Earth and, at the same time, aspirants to the heavens above, we can reverse that in a second and just decide to go along for the ride. It's an adventure. It's as fun as you make it. And when you play a game of it, balance, my friend, is restored. The heavy becomes light. The worrisome dissolves into laughter. And as the crème de la crème, you can give all the chaos cascades of love! Love helped create it and love helps you make it in our living a powerhouse of merriment and mirth, a carnival of laughter and a delight. "Glory be!" as the high beings say in Shinto, Tao and Christianity, and in the Glory Buddhist Temple of Lowell, Massachusetts. And for good measure, when the tech demands seem on overload and it's not funny anymore, do this. Take a slow breath. Rest the body. Quiet the mind. Nourish the spirit. And feel the love. Right within you now.

Stories are beginning to proliferate of people taking breaks from all things tech. You hear it in companies, on media, in families with kids on phones, in university classes and elementary schools, and with individual people who are fed up with society's obsession and focus on technical devices. Its common sense. And there is growing academic research which shows that excessive media use is not good for us physically, mentally, or emotionally.

Dr. Mary E. Gomes, professor of psychology at Sonoma State University, has assigned a four-day media fast for all her classes for years (a screen-free week is available online for anyone at www.screenfree.org). She has seen firsthand the benefits: being aware in the present moment (I say that the moment you lose your focus is when you lose your balance), better sleep, deeper connections, better productivity and learning, and breaking the tech habit which can inherently be a self-reinforcing pattern. Taking a media break is a powerful way to improve everyone's wellbeing.

Being in balance is a literal as well as a figurative reality. I want to keep myself in balance in every way I know how, in order to have smoothly functioning housing for my spirit of life, infused with love. And I give ample time to keeping my spirit – that is the part of me that aspires to live in higher awareness and goodness and to be a fully loving and love-giving person, as balanced as possible in my every day, earthly life. And to be the love that I love to receive and to make love the mainspring of my life, springing into action, feeling the demands and knowing I can return to center in a heartbeat.

I think most humans have a desire for social interaction with family members and friends and others to feel cared about, to help conduct our business and tend to our practical needs in this material world. But we may have strong urges to balance that with solitude. Why does a fisherman want to fish alone, but to be with their own thoughts without interruption and to appreciate nature by one's self? And why does a busy mom crave time alone? To settle their run-away thoughts and get a break from the demands of people dependent on them. Our psyches long for it. A balance between a peopled, busy world and a time to think, feel, and be alone is in the prescription for health of all four bodies of, I dare say, almost every person on this earth.

Quietude gives opportunity to let go of any earthly concerns that might impede your awareness rising to a higher level. Contemplation and reflection can only thrive in solitude. And how can you realize in an even bigger way that the love you seek is already here, you are it, and it will always be? You don't *need* an infusion from someone else. Your own consciousness is power housed by love, which is the highest vibration of all.

At the same time, as people in their later years lose friends and family members to the eventual and inevitable passing from this earth, many studies show that a social network is vital to our seniors' health and longevity. Social interactions later on in life help extend a healthier and happy life. I think we might all wish for loving nourishment from others to the end of our days.

Suzanne Giesemann says in *The Awakened Way* to balance your head with your heart. I take that to mean all your head activity with thinking, calculating, problem solving and, making connections needs the balance of your heart's love, wisdom and kindness. You can better yourself in your earthly daily living and in your heavenly pursuits when you are steady on your feet, poised for your next move and in harmony with all of creation.

Wanting balance in my whole being, I center myself in meditation. Letting all thoughts go and relaxing into nothingness, while my body sits cross-legged on my bed, mat or chair in order to not doze in a nothing state, or meditating while walking around close-by lakes or on nature's paths, or standing on a metro-train with my hand holding the strap. It can be seconds or hours. I return to center when I have wavered off to tend to earthly needs. I am pulled this way and that with requests and desires and then I come back to center, in the eye of the storm, as in my present September 2018 hurricane season of the Carolina's, for calm and quiet. In my dance alone in my home space I leap and crouch and tip and stretch to the skies and all around, on and off center and then return to the core. It's secure and peaceful there. My point of balance allows me to rest my thoughts and feel the natural flow of life. I feel love present for my balanced being on this earth and I sense harmony with the soft, tender, nurturing sounds in my ears from a higher place.

John Wooden, the 'Wizard of Westwood,' with a reputation as the greatest NCAA basketball head coach of all time, said this: "Next to love, balance is the most important thing."

I'll go with that! And I'll add, "As a love-filled being, do I feel within me and in the knowing of my heart that all is in balance? Is that knowing of my heart moving me along on my path? Is it aligning me with the love inside and creating my divine essence spark of love? One of my grandsons tells me that he figures balance comes naturally. And I say to him that if the heart is no longer heavy and you let go of all the emotional, mental, physical and soul-ful pain, the body is smart enough to find its own way to equilibrium where healing can take place.

Let's all live our lives in balance and harmony. It's the best place to be. It's easy to feel out-of-sorts with emotional and physical pain and a surge of thoughts that are throwing you off. But, you and you alone are capable of letting all of it go and finding the center of existence within yourself. That center core is where you find your balance. Calm and accord and peace are restored. And, bless the stars, with peace comes freedom! There are no weights to carry you down or concerns to rile you up. Just take off like the birds on a waft of air, perfectly balanced to fly to wherever your spirit leads.

Chapter 6

BIG

Immunity

Immunity, my second BIG health influence, is an innate powerhouse, a condition, a defense and an ability and protection that we all have and also acquire to varying degrees, to ward off, resist, act against or even be at truce or live amiably with, challenge, get rid of and overcome anything with the possibility of harm.

There are a host of potential pathogens including four major types of germs: bacteria, viruses, fungi, and protists (such as malaria and sleeping sickness via a bite from the tsetse fly) and being exposed to unknown, unkind forces. Cancer cells, parasites, toxic substances, diseases, insults, impacts, invasions, can all be threats to the life and health of all four of our emotional, mental, physical and spiritual bodies. The immune system is a network of cells, tissues, and organs that work together to defend and protect the body from assault.

White blood cells called leukocytes are our immunity cells, made in our bone marrow and stored in our blood and lymphatic tissue, and flowing through our blood stream. They are the key to resisting most any disease. Granulocytes help wounds by cleaning up debris after injury and preventing infections by killing germs in your body. Monocytes surround and destroy bacteria and viruses that might cause us harm. Let's admit it; we're at continual war with invaders.

That seems to be in conflict with love! Is war with things that make us sick and perhaps kill us incompatible with the biggest force of love and thus an oxymoron? Short answer is this: The energy of love and its creation is INFINITE! There is no beginning and no end. Love is everywhere. It puts an end to any negative forces out there or in here in our bodies by making impotent what can harm. We have free will to choose our own paths and to do with illness what we will. Remember that what is ill to one might be of no consequence and even a gift to another. Just as a gut bacterium growing in your gut might be beneficial in many ways to our digestion but if their composition is altered by antibiotics, illness or lifestyle, then that altered bacteria may cause many chronic diseases, such as inflammatory bowel disease, obesity, cancer, and autism.

And when a disease shows up we are free spirits to BE whatever we choose to be – positive, inspired to write that book while there's still time, energized, driven to support and find a cure. Anything is possible! There are no limits to spirit rising to any occasion. Love yourself and love others who are sharing this earthly space, as NOW is all we have. Just BE LOVE.

Immunity is a strong factor in maintaining overall health. Without our even knowing it, our body's immune system is in action around the clock to ward off interlopers, that could impede our normal healthy, balanced way of being. Unawares, we go about our day, mixing with crowds of people on public transportation, waiting appointments in waiting rooms, working and mixing with colleagues in the work place, being with children in schools as parents and teachers, and almost unconsciously exposing ourselves to the unknown.

Babies are in a particularly vulnerable spot, entering this world with an immature immunity. They do inherit some immunity genes through their two parent's genetic lines. But their immunity mainly builds over time with slow exposure to foreign substances. At the same time, babies have the benefit of their mother's antibodies (variable depending on the mother's immunity) being passed on through the placenta and the good bacteria in the vagina to grow a colony in the baby's gut for immunity. This lasts for a few months, as the baby is slowly exposed to harmful agents while building up their immunity even more. Breast milk gives added protection since it is filled with the mother's own antibodies and probiotics. Studies have shown that these babies have fewer infections and recover faster than babies who do not get breast milk. It's the best if you can breast feed - its nature's way, but if not, infant formula is a healthy alternative, filled with the best known nutrient combinations today. Starting pureed vegetables and fruits half-way into a baby's first year should keep the immune system healthy. But, know that breast milk does not protect a baby from some life-threatening infections like polio, diphtheria or measles.

Vaccination causes an immune response like bacteria or a virus would be a call to the troops of microphages (immune cells that are made in the bone marrow and travel to tissues in the body) in the blood. So, vaccination wards off the very serious diseases with a timed schedule of shots for babies to be immunized into their toddler years. And stats show that they do the job, though vaccinating the young is still controversial. Most adults in the industrialized nations have been vaccinated against many diseases and it pays off for the most part in health and lack of plagues and pandemics.

There are innate protections that come with our gift of a body in this material world. The skin for one, the largest organ in the body, keeps most invaders out. Secretions, mucous, bile, gastric acid, saliva, tears, and sweat serve us as defense mechanisms, ridding us of toxins, dross (foreign matter) and detritus (remains of oxidation), that get in the way of healthy functioning.

Other natural gatekeepers are the gastrointestinal tract, the respiratory tract, body hair, eyelashes, the nasopharynx, and cilia. The cilia that are motile or moving are in the lungs, respiratory tract and middle ear and with a waving action they keep our airways clear of mucus and dirt and they also propel sperm. Non-motile or primary cilia work as sensory antenna for the cell and are found in nearly every cell of the body, giving and receiving signals to and from other cells or fluids nearby. In the eye, non-motile cilia are found inside the retinal photoreceptors and with signaling, they allow the transport of vital molecules from one end of the photoreceptor to the other. The kidney cilia bend with urine flow and signal other cells that there is a flow. Giving and receiving a plethora of information from cell to cell throughout the body is vital to keep our immune system working optimally, with almost instant data on the status of all body cells. Intelligent work is going on every moment throughout our body to alert us to what might ail us or do us in. Knowing that our own body is protecting our own body should be a life-long comfort to our body and state of emotions, mind and spirit. That's called 'Loving Yourself!'

White blood cells, spoken of earlier, including monocytes, lymphocytes, neutrophils, basophils and eosinophils, are all on the front lines of our immune system to fight off infections. Bone marrow makes white blood cells, red blood cells and platelets, all important in immune action, and stores the blood cells in bone marrow and lymphatic tissues.

There are a lot of diseases and conditions that may affect white blood cell levels and compromise our immunity. Here are a few. Infections like urethritis, syphilis, encephalitis (inflammation of meninges surrounding brain and spinal cord) and sepsis (systemic infection leading to immune system meltdown with organ damage, failure and death) are all tied in with a higher-than-normal white blood cell count, multiplying of the cells to destroy an enemy, such as a virus or bacteria.

Leukemia and lymphoma are cancers of the blood causing uncontrolled growth of an abnormal type of blood cell in the bone marrow and impairment of the ability of the bone marrow to produce red blood cells and platelets, resulting in an increased risk of infection and bleeding. The immune system is being attacked to the core.

Myelodysplastic syndrome is a type of cancer, in which some cells in the bone marrow are or become abnormal or dysplastic and have trouble making new blood cells. Another immune condition is myeloproliferative disorder. It triggers the excessive production of immature blood cells, resulting in an unhealthy balance of all types of blood cells in the bone marrow and too many or too few white blood cells in the blood.

What is the treatment for these cancers? Radiation, surgery and chemotherapy have been and are the main tools in the tool box for cancers. But, you know there is this bug-a-boo. Besides the illness itself, medicines, that are meant to heal and cure, can still treat us as badly as the disease. Though there are drugs to alleviate nausea, chemo can make you very sick, as well as raise or lower the body's white blood cell count and thus your immunity, which is not a good thing if it's off the normal range.

And there is this to watch out for. Sometimes prescribed drugs interact in the body's system and can kill. It happened with the wife of Jonathan Santlofer, author of *The Widower's Notebook*. It took a couple of days of illness building up and not taken seriously by the medics and suddenly she couldn't breath and died. Her immune system was of no help with drugs in conflict with one another.

A high (on or above the range) white blood cell count could also mean you are fighting a viral or bacterial infection, are reacting to a drug such as corticosteroids or epinephrine, have a disease of bone marrow like myelofibrosis, have chronic lymphatic leukemia or chronic myelogenous leukemia or have acute lymphocytic leukemia or acute myelogenous leukemia, or have rheumatoid arthritis, are a smoker, engage in extreme exercise, are experiencing common ailments such as colds and flu, are feeling heavy emotional or physical stress and many other threats to well-being.. They all raise your white blood cell count higher than it should be and that information then is an indicator of those specific diseases. Those white blood cells are hugely important when talking immune disorders and could be the 'mascot' or poster child for the importance of immunity. Let's keep those cells talking to each other!

Then we have the HIV and AIDS virus that is prominent in our public awareness and discourse. HIV, human immunodeficiency virus, is a retrovirus (composed of RNA, not DNA) that infects and kills blood cells, known as CD4 T-cells. As those cells are wiped out over time, the body is less able to defend itself, even against common illnesses. When HIV has fully compromised the immune system and the body is open to deadly diseases known as opportunistic infections, we call it AIDS for acquired immunodeficiency syndrome. HIV acts as the cause and AIDS is the effect of such infection. The normal count range of white blood cells called CD4 cell, is 500-1500. The higher the number you have within that range, the better it is for immunity. When it drops below 200, a person is diagnosed with AIDS. Combinations of antiretroviral drugs or ARV are given to reduce the size of the virus load and to slow the action of the virus in your blood and body fluids. That slows down the HIV disease and people are living for many years while taking the cocktail of medicines for the rest of their lives. There are serious side effects, but generally they are manageable.

But, the recurring reality is that no cure has been found for HIV/AIDS or most any other immune disorder. We haven't conceived or created a way to bring the body back to managing all the blood counts in a normal way or to reset our immune system to working splendidly as nature intended. The dream is to make order out of dis-order. Not to repress or damp down nor to do a half-fix, but to find what will cure and restore our immunity to health.

Elton John, world-famous musician and indomitable advocate for reducing the stigma of AIDS and of supporting AIDS research to find a cure, has his own prescription for health. The title of his book, *LOVE is the CURE* © 2012, gives it away. He had many friends who died of AIDS in the '80s and he is determined to stop its spread. Elton says in his book that the disease must be cured not by a miraculous vaccine but by changing hearts and minds and through a collective effort to break down social barriers and to build bridges of compassion. When we treat people as worthy of love, their worth is realized for everyone to see. And ultimately that is the most powerful weapon we have against stigma and against AIDS. Elton John's life and words do and say for us to treat everyone with dignity and compassion. He shares that many good things in his life wouldn't have happened but for love. "If you give love out, you get love back … It's the only thing that matters." His vision is that with love driving our actions we can end AIDS and we can build a better world.

And part of our better world, I say, is to muster up all the forces for good in the world of science. We're hunting for tangible tools and methods to build our immunity and to counteract the punch of pathological threats to the health of us all. Here are some examples of the medical research going on in the world of immune disorders.

One medical attempt at mimicking immunity's natural good sense is in immunotherapy. Also called biologic therapy, it uses your body's own immune system to help fight cancer and other debilitating diseases. The researchers take T-cells or messenger immunity cells, that are made by the body or engineered in a laboratory and injects them subcutaneously to initiate protective T-cell immunity. The cells can recognize, target and destroy cancer and other cells, while avoiding healthy cells and thus improve or restore immune system function.

Scientists are finding ways to tweak genes in the body's immune cells by using electrical fields. A 2018 preview issue of *Bioelectricity* reports that pulsed electric fields are helping fight cancer, whether by inducing tumor cell death or by stimulating the immune system. And In *Nature* July 11, 2018 scientists reported that a quick zap of electricity makes T cells more receptive to taking in new genetic material and gene-editing reagents. That speeds up the gene research which can make a big difference for someone with cancer.

As I am writing this in 2018, I am seeing more and more immunotherapy in mainstream medical offerings, a treatment that boosts the immune system, especially for cancer, with some supposed success. DISCOVER Jan/Feb 2012 reported that a new therapy turns leukemia patients' own cells into cancer assassins and that it might help fight other cancers, too. More lab work being done is to alter immune cells to block HIV and there are human trials going on as we speak. It took medical researchers, in my observation, a while to come back to the concept of your own body resources ability to resist unwanted invaders if you build up your immunity, If your immune system is exhausted you are vulnerable to most anything.

Some of the thinking is that inflammation, which can be pervasive throughout the body, triggers the autoimmunity in any auto-immune disease. Pollutants and chronic stress are factors in inflammation. Diet also, seems to be a factor in cause, so, if this rings true for you, avoid sugar, caffeine, starchy carbohydrates, dairy and foods with gluten. And, just for the oddness of doing it, let me give you just one of 100s of suggestions I could make to improve our health and this one is often overlooked. Zinc is the chemical element of atomic number 30, a silvery-white metal that is used for galvanizing iron and steel to protect against corrosion. Is there a metaphor here for zinc's protecting our immune system from corrosion? We humans need zinc for the eyes, for regulating sleep that is vital to restore our immunity and for supporting a strong immune system by healing wounds and zinc undergirds normal growth, making no room for the unwanted growth of viruses and bacteria. As a bonus, it helps with smelling and tasting. It is abundant on this earth but you need only a small amount to stay healthy and well. You can take it as a supplement or you can find it big time in my vegetarian diet: vegetables, spinach and nuts. Add to the zinc list cereal, wheat germ and mushrooms, and for others: meat, lobster and oysters. Zinc is just a sample of our many nutritional needs that I magnified for your attention. You can give the same attention on your own to dozens of other minerals and vitamins. They are best found in vital food but if you go for a supplement, Standard Process Laboratories in Wisconsin provides compressed food products, often including meat (caution vegetarians), loaded naturally with those vitamins and minerals that your body is asking for. Listen to your body. Are you listening?

Don't overdue any supplements. They contain amounts of enzymes, minerals, vitamins beyond what you find in the food we prepare. Your body has a delicate balance to maintain. It may just need a nudge of an enzyme or mineral to provide for a need. There is such a thing as too much of a good thing. The reports on turmeric infusion in 2017 preceding a death give us pause.

And beyond nutritional needs, for more good measure, if you're game for trying essential oils for well-being, I'll give you *Tea Tree* oil, one of many essential oils used for health. Add a drop to your diffuser or dab a drop on your wrist pulse, where you can feel the blood action close to the skin to quickly and easily absorb the healing scent. Tea tree oil is made to order for immunity concerns since it contains many compounds, including terpinen-4-ol, that are thought to deter and kill bacteria, viruses and fungi and to increase the white blood cell action to fight germs and other invaders. It's a natural remedy for treating bacterial and fungal skin conditions, preventing infection and promoting healing.

And we'll leave other many hundreds of nutrition and aroma tips for other needs, for other writings and for your using you own good common sense and wisdom.

Build up your immunity with whatever resonates with you and serves you well and, most importantly, give yourself love and keep it coming. Your body senses the consummate energy of love and responds with confidence to make you strong, resilient and vibrant. Those inter-cellular messages should and will be good ones!

It's a mystery why our immune system can go haywire. For mostly unknown reasons our very own cells, that seek to protect us from invaders that could disable and kill us, can go rogue and attack our own body. Auto-immune disorders are witness to that phenomenon.

And, here are a few more disorders, besides ones I have mentioned already, that fit in that category. Sjögren's syndrome, is a disorder of your immune system identified by its two most common symptoms — dry eyes and a dry mouth. The mucous membranes and moisture-secreting glands of your eyes and mouth are usually affected first, resulting in decreased tears and saliva. Treatment focuses on relieving symptoms. The condition, more common in women over age 40, as in multiple sclerosis, often accompanies other immune system disorders, such as rheumatoid arthritis and lupus. Why is that? It's enough of a puzzle to realize that the body can attack itself and more to wonder if you have one disease you might likely get another. To me, that would seem to indicate that a very strong attack team of our immune cells going rogue are disassembling the whole body framework supporting immunity. Our very own cells are turning against us and our defenses are way down.

Yes, the body, down to each individual cell is capable of making choices – good and bad! How we can influence those choices to be only good is still a puzzle. Or perhaps the answer is right before our eyes – love your body as yourself. Respect, care for, embrace, be aware of, connect in your mind's eye with every body cell and treat each and all with kindness. Sound too esoteric? Try it over time and see if it makes a difference in how you feel and how your measurements of health adjust to the embrace of love. Acknowledging and expressing kindness as a key manifestation of love can make the difference between deprivation and radiant health for all. Shirley MacClaine just sent me an alert that today, November 13, is World Kindness Day. Let's all be kind to ourselves in every way and spread that kindness to the world. When we get the feel of it, every day can be world kindness day!

Hashimotos's thyroiditis is also autoimmune. My husband developed this after he was found to have Addison's disease three decades ago, where the body attacks its own adrenal glands. That imbalance in Addison's adrenals leads to more imbalance in Hashimoto's thyroid where the body attacks its own thyroid gland. The whole endocrine system was under attack. Years after those took up residence in my husband's body, in the late-1990s, the normal cells of my husband's esophagus became abnormal as in Barrett's Esophagus, and then became cancerous. It was an attack he could not sustain and his body gave in and, so sadly for me and our children and grandchildren, he died in January 1997. Am I implying that his cancer was due to all the imbalances of his immune system going haywire with Addison's and Hashimoto's? I think his immune system attacking parts of his own body was a strong factor in his not being able to stop the cancerous growth progression that wracked his used-to-be healthy, beautiful physical frame.

To name (in alphabetical order just for the pleasure of having some order in our lives) just a few more auto-immune disorders of the 100 plus known ones are celiac disease, where eating gluten can damage the small intestine, and was brought to public awareness with TV's *Survivor* and TV host Elisabeth Hasselbeck's book, *The G-Free Diet.* Crohn's disease is a severe and persistent inflammation of the bowel, which a concert pianist relative of mine lived uncomfortably with for many years, as she continued to perform and teach. Endometriosis is a disease, where the tissue that normally lines a woman's uterus grows somewhere else. That imbalance of auto-immunity can create havoc, including the inability to get pregnant. Juvenile arthritis, which I was on the cusp of having at age 16, my senior year of high school and I wrote about in my first book, *The Cheshire Cat Syndrome, My Adventure With Arthritis* © 1996, is auto-immune as well as its relative, rheumatoid arthritis, in adults. Myasthenia gravis, or ALS, a most serious auto-immune disease by any measure, relentlessly and progressively renders loss of movement and function in musculature throughout the body and usually ultimately shuts it down totally with the inability to breath.

Even in that most 'threatening to normalcy' of diseases, when the death knoll is ticking, love can make a difference. I know of someone with

ALS who was ready to die. She was on breathing equipment, could not use the muscles in much of her body, including her muscles for speech, and she wanted to leave her body behind. Her husband understood her eye signals, yes and no, to want to invite their friends and family to a party to celebrate her life with them and say goodbye. They all gathered and showered her with their love, telling her stories of their beautiful times together and their caring for her. One after another each one thanked her, praised her for who she was, and embraced her with hearts full with love. After the party, things changed for her. Her husband asked her and got an eye signal yes or no, did she want to keep living? Yes, she had changed her mind. Her spirit was raised. She went on to live for two more years, appreciating each moment. Love can add years to your life and your spirit can reach for the stars! This woman, Dewie, was the wife of Pete Quortrup, the President of the ALS Living Fund, whose mission is to help people living with ALS. He is a friend and I know that love fills his heart, with a story to tell.

Another auto-immune disease is narcolepsy, a brain disorder that, though very serious, seems a little more innocent midst the life-threatening diseases I've spoken of. It involves poor control of sleep-wake cycles. Dreams might be hit or miss, but they are important to have for the brain to do its sleep time cleanout work of ridding the clutter of thoughts. Don't be fearful of bad dreams since they are a time to process the painful experiences of our day and that's a good thing. Fear, guilt and shame are released in dreams and you can be the healthier for it. And look for premonitions, messages and creative ideas to inspire. Releasing anguish and seeing the hope might just help your consciousness to settle into a lengthier sleep cycle. Here's a suggestion from me for insomnia, without obvious cause. Before you fall asleep think love. Feel the embrace in your heart from someone you love and hear their saying, "I love you." Feel a vibration of warmth and caring surround you and fill you. When sleep fades away, let gratitude be your awakening.

Optic neuritis is inflammation of the optic nerve that usually resolves by itself in time. Rheumatic fever, another inflammatory auto-immune disorder, is a complication that can develop after a Streptococcus bacterial infection, more commonly known as strep throat. Vasculitis, acute or chronic, manifests as inflammation of the blood vessels, causing thickening, weakening, narrowing or scarring of the blood vessel walls, which in turn restrict blood flow and can result in organ and tissue damage.

So you can see there are a host of places and ways and degrees of impact in and on the body that each cell of the body might choose to attack itself.

A well-functioning immune system is a life or death matter. We don't know why some people succumb or why our cells go rogue or what to do about it. But an immersion in love can only be for the good. Love conquers all, from perhaps extending your estimated time left on this earth, to making that time the joy of your life. The warmth of that love will melt away your stress and transport you to heights you have not yet been.

David Felten, a neuroscientist, at the University of Rochester, along with two colleagues, Bob Ader (died in 2011) and Nicholas Cohen, founded a field of research called *psychoneuroimmunology*. They learned in their research that in protecting us from illness, the brain and the immune system work together. They discovered a complex web of connections. First they found the hard-wired nerve connections. Then they found receptors for the neurotransmitters produced by the brain – on the surface of immune cells, as well as finding new neurotransmitters that could talk to those cells, with the lines of communication going in both directions. Psychological factors such as stress can trigger the release of neurotransmitters which influences an immune response. And the chemicals released by the immune system can in turn influence the brain, triggering, as an example, the tiredness and fever of illness.

I want to exclaim, "Yes! We've known the brain and the immune system are connected from our own experience!" But, of course we need scientific data to prove what we suspect is so and they came up with it.

This gives us even more room to speculate on what thoughts can we think and what feelings can we emote to get our immune system back on track and to do completely what is best for our health. Working half-way for our health and then going into a state of rebellion and attacking itself is a detriment to the state of well-being of all our bodies and is a disservice to the good work that they do.

Instead of thinking the body is attacking itself, just think, I love my body. I see each cell of every organ, tissue and fluid getting along, talking to each other, knowing what each other needs, and cooperating in an ongoing, continuous kinship. I feel my whole body as one and that unified being is what I am. Loving your body might make you stronger to resist an auto-immune take-over of your body cells. Love conquers all!

Psychological factors can also mean our feelings of rejection, abandonment, hurt, shame, anxiety and loneliness. If that can affect our immune system, then let's let love full of compassion, caring, attentiveness, tenderness, warmth and kindness fill our coffers to overflowing and we'll see what Love hath wrought. Love may well persuade our immune system to stop the sabotage. Let's give ourselves a caress in gratefulness. Our bodies have our sanction to return to a balanced state of radiant health, whenever the body is ready to heal itself.

Chapter 7

BIG

Genetics

Genetics, my third BIG health influence, gives your body, mind and emotions the map to differentiate your embryonic cells into organs, nerves, bones and other body tissue and to thus create all parts of you and influence your growth and your demise. That's BIG! And to qualify this miracle production right at the start, as we have learned increasingly more and more about our genes, we know they are not the total be all and end all to pass on traits. There is wiggle room in finding that some genes that might likely cause breast cancer or pass on a neurological disorder need to be triggered. And the potential for triggering a gene to express or not may be passed on genetically, too. Also, one gene from one parent may have a stronger or a lesser influence that the partner gene, coming from the other parent, on that corkscrew chain of a chromosome. We don't know why that happens. There is much to consider in realizing the importance of our genes and genetic history to our health.

If there is a chance of influencing these imbalances in gene expression for the good, we have opportunity to enlist all of the energies we can muster to recognize, repair, reenergize and restore our healthful state of being. Love is at the top of the list! Love is the all-encompassing power of the highest vibration, an energy that overrides all others to make us whole again. Try it! For the known as well as the unknown in our genetic make-up.

Before I go further into the many facets of genetics that influence our health, here's a good dose of hope to inoculate you against potential despair.

The front page story, *Gene Therapy Targets Canavan Disease,* written by Doug Steinberg, in the September 17, 2001 issue of *The Scientist,* a magazine for life science professionals and published in Ontario, Canada, brings up the gene therapy research being done then on a group of young patients with Canavan disease. Max Randell was one of those very young patients.

Canavan disease is a genetic, neurodegenerative disorder. Each of the two parents of an infant with Canavan disease carries one copy of a mutated gene, but probably do not themselves have the disease. The infant might be limp and listless and over time, never walk or talk, maybe leading to an early death. The intellect can stay sharp but with little way to express it. Their facial expressions and responses show an uncanny awareness, maybe laughing when you do something funny or moving their fingers when you are playing the piano. There is a lack of an enzyme ASPA which means that the white matter in the brain turns spongy because no myelin is being produced. The nerves need the protective covering of myelin to function normally. Gene therapy injects the ASPA gene into the brain that helps the brain neurons to secrete the ASPA that allows the production of myelin to surround and protect the nerves.

Max Randell, at age 11 months, had his first of two gene therapy deliveries of genes to his brain, to improve his vision and his mobility.

Max's story, along with his disease-free brother, Alex Randell, who is five years younger than Max, is reported by Ricki Lewis, PhD on a

December 5, 2013 post on DNA Science Blog and entitled, "A Brother's Love Fights Genetic Disease." That love, with the stakes so high, should get our attention!

Alex felt such love for his big brother. Max was around five when he and the infant Alex would lay on a bed together with their faces pressed into each other and eyes looking directly into each other's eyes. I've seen the pictures. Out of love, Alex has cared for his brother in many ways and then taking over more and more, helping to meet all his needs. At age 2 ½ years, Alex was stuffing envelopes and giving 'speeches' to help raise money for research, reading to Max as soon as Alex could read, researching genetic therapy at age ten and following through with reaching out to scientists about scientific study of Canavan Disease and what are we doing about it for others and for Max. And their mother, Ilyce, who has done everything she could for Max and Alex with gratefulness and love, feels their love and comfort in return. When sitting on the sofa and reading a gene therapy book, that she had written, to Max who was lying down next to her, she started crying. Max managed to reach his little hand to grab her arm. He looked directly in her eyes with comfort, and seeming to say he's okay with his life, he's happy. She's hoping that people can see all the happiness and love that children like her Maxie bring to the world.

The last I knew over a year ago, was that Max has gained some eyesight, mobility and verbal ability steadily from the time of his gene therapy. That means the genes injected into his brain are still alive and working. He graduated from high school at age 19. He smiles and is happy. Everyone is grateful for the treatments because of the progress he has made.

Alex and Max are bonded in love for a lifetime and their love goes both ways. And, as if that weren't enough, the family likes to talk about Max's "healing powers." They say that when someone isn't feeling well in the family they ask him to use his healing powers and he begins to laugh and in a couple of hours the person feels better. They can't explain it but it's just there.

Fewer than 1,000 people in the US are known to have Canavan disease, usually Ashkenazi Jews and a few in other ethnic groups. But the impact of genetic therapy research, that the Randell's had a part in, goes beyond Canavan disease and could affect many more people and inform other genetic neurodegenerative disease research. And to make a good situation even better, Alex plans to be a neuroscientist. Their abundant love is having an impact in many ways.

So, with that story of hope and love in the world of genetic disorders to fortify you, we can explore even more facets of genetics that influence our health to remind, learn, have our own ideas about, see the potential and comment on.

Let's review the making of a human. Right from the moment of conception, the gene endowed sperm and gene endowed egg – each sperm and egg with only 23 chromosomes or half the number of chromosomes that are needed to make a human, come together, unite, are joined as 23 pairs of chromosomes. They make a unique, full chain count of 46 chromosomes, each containing hundreds to thousands of genes that are laced on the chromosomes. Each chromosome of a pair has two strands of DNA, the cell's genetic material that is contained in chromosomes, tightly coiled around proteins or histones that serve as a support for the DNA's structure and that spiral in a double helix. The chromosomes thread their long way through the nucleus of each divided cell. A gene, the main subject of our concern in genetics for health, is a segment of that DNA and passes down from parents to children to confer a trait or traits to the offspring. There are around 25,000 genes in each cell of the human body and that makes for a big blueprint for our finite frame and each gene coming with instructions on how it operates. Each gene provides a code to make a protein that will determine the traits of who you are. Some traits are controlled by many genes that act together. Genes might act as recessive, needing both genes in the gene pair to express a trait. Dominant traits are controlled by one gene of a pair of chromosomes. Once fertilization has taken place the all-important production of new cells begins. Dividing, dividing to create new cells for the rest of your life. *Mitosis*, a process for growth and asexual reproduction, has the biggest, continuous job of creating all somatic or body cells throughout our bodies during a lifetime and it ignites in a flash. *Melosis*, a process that focuses on reproduction, producing gametes (sperm and egg cells or germ cells) for sexual propagation, fades out over time with menopause and sperm count dwindling. Two gametes fuse to form a zygote, a cell with the full number of chromosomes, each of our 'selves,' and we are off and running. The reproduction of all body and germ cells has begun in the first sparkle and flare of a new life.

Now that we've spelled out and reminded ourselves of the genetic process taking place in creation of life, we can better picture happenings, understand and maybe figure out how to have healing and know what is going on and what to do about it, if and when something goes wrong again. That gives us a gleam of understanding of what takes place to create body cells and the genes that help run the show. So let's take it from there.

Most of everyone's personal characteristics – height, eye color, fine textured hair, teeth resistant to decay, a recognizable gait, a happy disposition and freckles can be at least partly determined by your genes. It takes two to tango, thanks to both parents, for a lot of how you look and act and feel. Musical ability can come as a package of several genetic traits – one for acute hearing to help determine pitch, one for finger agility, and other genes for music perception and music memory. There are quirky traits such as ears that wiggle and thumbs that you can bend way back, that come through the gene traits you inherit, more likely from one parent as a dominant trait or as a recessive trait combined with a recessive gene in the other parent to make a zygote that becomes a newborn offspring. A predisposition to diseases or the disease itself can be passed on from one or both parents and to male or female children or to both. As an example, a change in one gene passed on from one parent can cause sickle cell anemia in the progeny.

And here's a mouthful of another genetic disorder. All people who have only a single copy of the normal FGFR3 gene from one parent and a single copy of the FGFR3 gene mutation from the other parent have achondroplasia. Achondroplasia (repeating strengthens the memory!) is a disorder of bone growth with disproportionate short stature and accompanying breathing problems and obesity. It is the most common type of dwarfism.

And there is this to add to the mix. Acquired (or somatic) mutations occur during a person's life and are present only in some body cells. Genes can be damaged if an error is made as DNA copies itself during cell division or damaged by exposure to the sun's ultraviolet radiation, toxic chemicals and other environmental agents that cause the DNA to break down. So here we can be proactive! Be diligent to avoid all toxins, radiation and anything that might harm the genes that we started with on this earthly trip. Protecting ourselves from danger is self-love in its most admirable form.

Hereditary Hemochromatosis or HH causes the body to absorb too much iron which in turn, causes severe organ damage if untreated. A child who inherits two copies of a mutated gene, one from each parent, is very likely to get the disease. If only one mutated HH gene is inherited you are a carrier and may possibly pass on the trait, and you will probably not experience any symptoms since only one good gene can take care of regulating iron absorption. One good gene can carry the load. Carriers are more likely to show signs of HH if there are triggers such as diabetes or alcoholism. A significant 10 percent of the U.S. population carries the gene. The treatment is to remove blood (phlebotomy) from the patient in order to lower the overall level of iron in the blood. This can be a notice for us to make good choices in our consumption of food or drink and by avoiding things that can lead to addictions.

Triggers can provoke a wayward gene into action to our detriment. But, life provides that we aren't necessarily given a life sentence with our inheritance of genetic material. We can be proactive to stay in the best of health and not to set off a sleeping, damaging gene with our behavior. As my mother used to say about smoking – and no one in our family or church or close friends smoked, "If God wanted you to smoke he would have put a chimney on your head."

Mahtob Mahmoody, author of *My Name is Mahtob* © 2015, at age 6, escaped Iran with her mother, Betty Mahmoody, author of the bestseller, *Not Without My Daughter* © 1987, and made into a movie, from her father's (also her mother's husband's) abusive imprisoning. Mahtob suffered much stress and fear of abduction for many years in the U.S. until she heard of her father's death. She developed lupus erythematosus as a teen, with periodic severe episodes. I have spoken in past pages of systemic lupus erythematosus or SLE as an autoimmune disease, with a wide range of symptoms, but it also is considered a complex genetic disorder. The disease tends to occur in families. When Mahtob was a University student, she resolved many issues and in her own heart she forgave her father. She faced her fears and was freed from their power. She learned of the lethal impact of hatred on our lives and our souls and she let go of hate. She found comfort and wisdom in her protestant religion. She altered her life by changing her attitude. Remember, dear readers, that the opposite of the shackles of fear is LOVE. The power of love overwhelms and dissipates fear. Mahtob felt better and better physically and got test results to show that her lupus was in full remission. I don't know what her status is now in 2018, but she has let go of all her heavy emotional weights of the past and she continues to nurture her spirit. That speaks to me of love. She is not afraid to love.

So, you can see that there are many variables in diseases and syndromes that one can inherit from their parents and with varying manifestations of the disease. And questions are raised. What can we do with genetics on a broad scale to prevent illnesses? Can we intervene to stop or slow any showing up of a disease and/or its symptoms?

Getting at the gene itself is where the urges are. Medical researchers are looking for ways to damp down or to do away with the aberrant gene's power. And here are mentions of what's being done. Scientists are editing DNA in human embryos to fix a disease gene (published in *Nature* and reported on *All Things Considered* by Rob Stein 8.2.17), that would ultimately help families plagued by genetic diseases, such as heart disorders, Huntington's disease, Alzheimer's, breast and ovarian cancer, and cystic fibrosis. Research in genetics is loaded with ethical issues and this is no exception. But until it reaches the 'make a baby stage' research will probably move along.

Science researchers are not just editing, but are removing genes from white blood cells of the immune system and inserting beneficial replacements. When the studies can be replicated in more than one laboratory it might make its way to benefiting a host of diseases, including HIV, lupus, rheumatoid arthritis, and cancer. But, they have a long way to go before they are ready for mainstream treatment.

In the meantime, what do we do? Medical offerings will keep improving, but generally not with a 'cure.' Alternative treatments will become more available and affordable. The public, that is you, is better informed every day and is more open than ever to a plethora of health workers out there with healing offerings.

May love come to the rescue! How could the energy of love not be a help to keep those genes in a quiet place with no need to express? Body, mind and emotions that are filled with love, I think might counter the baser energy of disease. Love expressed! And good news, according to studies published in the November 2012 journal, *Frontiers in Genetics*, we also have protective genes that help centenarians live into their 100's, in spite of having as many disease-associated genes as other people. The good genes are expressed and the disease genes are put to rest.

In continuing genetic studies done in 2011 and earlier at the Salk Institute of California, skin cells are taken from schizophrenia patients and, thanks to state-of –the-art technology, are transformed into functional neurons. Drugs are tested on these neurons and the best one wins to be the most likely one to help the patients with this prevalent psychiatric disorder.

Gene therapy may soon help the body to produce its own insulin in diabetes.

In the plant kingdom, GMOs or genetically modified organisms alter plant seeds to resist disease, pests, weed killers and to better survive draught. Their safety for consuming has been and still is under question and now you see many food labels that say No GMOs. If you want to take less chance of consuming food that could harm you, look for the label 'Organic.'

Multiply those studies to know that much research work is happening in many areas of disease and well-being that could improve our health on a lot of fronts.

Genetics is a big influence on our health in so many ways and our knowledge is growing at a fast clip. The more we learn the wider the genetic field becomes with new choices to be made that can all impact our health and wellbeing. And, we have lots of opportunity to examine 'what does love have to do with it?'

Here is an ethically controversial practice that is being done today. A person with a genetic disease can pass that gene on to their children. Medical researchers are in the early stages of coming out of research and removing or editing that gene from the chromosome in human sperm, eggs, and embryos of a parent to be requesting it. If they remove it from an egg, they then put the sperm and egg together in a petri dish and a human being is hatched. The embryo is frozen and saved until the parent decides to have it inserted in her or another's uterus, to gestate and give birth to a child who, they are relieved to have known, does not carry the mutated gene. Other parents will take a chance and know that it's possible their child will inherit the aberrant gene and be ill in the future and perhaps die. It is controversial because a host of people believe this is tampering with life and we should leave that in the hands of a higher power.

But, in addressing love, with new human beings under the microscope, chances are those children, where the disease gene presence is unknown, will be loved fully and fervently whether the child has the gene or not and if the gene is present they will likely feel it is a 'God-given' part of who they are – I've heard kids and parents say this from the heart. And the children who had the gene removed in the egg or zygote stage of their development will be just as loved for all the things they are and have parents grateful for knowing that their child is free of the disease and will never pass it on.

I bring it up for our knowing that this is a growing reality in genetics today and it will only increase in use with more genes being discovered that cause illness and maybe death and with more exact techniques for more successful procedures. There are strong beliefs on either side of this issue and children are being born with parents knowing or not knowing that their baby got or not the gene no one wants. There is so much love here either way and we can be grateful for the presence of love. Love that a wanted child is brought into this world to be nourished and loved and teach us lessons and love us in return. I think most of us have heard something of this from parents of kids with Down syndrome (an extra copy of chromosome 21 is present), and an array of genetic disorders and intrauterine fetal damage like cerebral palsy.

I remember United States Vice President (from 1965 to 1969) Hubert Humphrey, back in the 1970s, speaking about his granddaughter Vicky, born with Down's syndrome, showing that he adored her, taking her on walks and saying that they have seen what can be done with love - and it takes a lot of love, he offered. He called the love that comes back God's true love and it really and truly is. He gets more joy out of their little Vicky than almost any experience that he's ever had or any child he's ever known. What a statement he gave on the beauty of love! Our long ago VP honored her by working tirelessly for equal treatment for people with disabilities. And Vicky's sister Jill said that they truly felt she was their sunshine. All that love certainly healed hearts if any needed healing. That deep, rich love, given and received, was spread to countless others, including me to read about in the newspapers decades ago and to feel the love in my heart.

I delight in the 'grocery baggers' with Down's syndrome who are hired and working at my local chain grocery store and I honestly feel LOVE going both ways with a few kind words. That really makes the world a better place. So, love fills the coffers of our hearts, from a spectrum of players on this planet. Try not to miss a thing. Love is moving in waves right now and you might catch a wave if you can!

Cystic fibrosis is caused by a gene that tells the body to produce thick mucus in the lungs and digestive system that results in infections and difficulty absorbing nutrients. The gene mutation has to come from both parents to cause the disease. By studying the gene sequence researchers are finding new ways to treat it.

Mutations in genes may cause a cancer cell to multiply without stopping. We have been able to modify that growth with chemicals but it's not perfect and research has been going on for decades.

Cancer develops when DNA is damaged or changed by chemicals, radiation, microbes, etc. It can grow in almost any tissue and, as my homoeopathist said 25 years ago, especially in reproductive tissue. The American Cancer Society says that you have a 1 in 3 chance of contracting cancer in your lifetime and a 1 in 5 chance of dying from it. Cancer in the U.S. is the second biggest cause of death (heart disease is #1). Decades of research have focused mostly on drugs to stop the growth of these aberrant cells. That means chemotherapy, radiation, hormonal therapy, and surgery. Genetics are used to target specific cancer cells more accurately, that being the genetic signature of each patient's tumor. We have moved from organ-focused (as in prostate cancer or stomach cancer) to a gene-focused approach. So, where does that leave us? The medical route does work for many people to halt or delay further growth, but with sickness and sometimes death happening along the way. Alternative and more natural therapies are pursued by many with some success and even bringing miraculous cures and may be used alone or in conjunction with traditional medical treatments.

It's a tough call. Rampant with risk. And whatever the choices made by the diagnosed, it is a brave choice, and many times if not most, totally changes a person's approach to life and often for the good. Life can become more meaningful, less important things are let go of, and relationships become more filled with caring and yes, LOVE. And that's a good thing. Whether or not you can stay alive or even extend your lifetime, life itself becomes more meaningful and precious. You are 'being' in every moment, a gift that the higher powers have given you. And this all-body-change can work for any health challenge we face.

I am! And the support of that is love and that brings together and encompasses all that we know. Each of our stories, as important, touching and heart rending as they present, are superseded by love. Be! Know! Love! That is ALL there is, dear friends!

Chapter 8

What's Your Heart Got to Do with It?

The heart is the center of it all. Love resides here at the core. In your physical body your heart-modeled heart is front and center. Your chest pulses with the vibration of the heart for a lifetime. Emotions fill every heart chamber and cell and are stored to surface in a flash, set off with a heart-touching prompt and filling you with longing, or fear and regret, as well as joy. Love overtakes them all. Your intelligence of heart-mind is sparking every one of the 40,000 neurons in the heart that transmit messages to and from the brain, lungs and other organs. Like the heart-brain that it is, it can sense, feel, learn and remember. Let's call it a smart heart!

This fist-sized muscle is pumping blood, without let-up, carrying a load of oxygen, nutrients and hormones for the heart's own sake as well as to the furthest reaches of our body cells and organs and then returns to expel carbon dioxide or CO_2 via the lungs and to dispel metabolic wastes along the way. Oxygen or O helps burn the fuel in our cells to produce energy. That's what we run on, fellow mortals, and there would be no running, only death if oxygen vanished from our lungs and from this earth. Oxygen is our most important element to breathe and thus live and besides, we're made of it. Water is vital, too. Over half of our body consists of water or H_2O, each molecule containing two hydrogen atoms bonded to one oxygen atom. With variables you can live 3 minutes without air, 3 days without water, and 3 weeks without food. Oxygen is vital for respiration in most living organisms. In our atmosphere there is an abundant supply of oxygen for respiration, produced by plants through photosynthesis. And oxygen is a biomarker for life on extrasolar planets. This #8 element on the Periodic Table of Elements is of utmost importance. We can be grateful to and from our hearts for oxygen being a major player in our health and on the front lines for life. Please, save a big place for gratefulness. Saying thank you and meaning it with all your heart does wonders for the recipient of your loving attention, including your own heart, and for you all to feel the glow of radiant health for your physical body, your emotional state, your spirit and your mind. And, I would say, the heart has all four bodies wrapped up in one amazing instrument of love.

As food is digested in the gastro-intestinal tract, blood flows through intestinal capillaries and picks up glucose, vitamins, and minerals to be passed along wherever they are needed. With blood flowing and the vessels of arteries, veins and capillaries pulsing and heart pumping, the circulatory or vascular system tracks a 100,000 mile long network of blood vessels throughout this grown up physical body. Waste from the body tissues is filtered out from the blood as it flows through the kidneys to make urine and to be excreted to nourish and recycle life's leftovers to the bowels of the earth. Your feces comes from bile, the fluid made in the liver and secreted into your intestines to help digest fat and also comes as a byproduct of the broken down hemoglobin in old and damaged red blood cells. The feces is expelled through the rectum and anus. Good riddance for the light-hearted.

The vascular system knows about nourishing and about waste. It gets rid of what no longer serves the needs of our working bodies. How wise it is to let go of unneeded weights. In our day-to-day lives, an emotional weight can take you down to a low level of functioning. It's hard to find love there.

Our heart operates with electrical and chemical signals that can become disturbed. The rhythm of a heart can lose its evenness and steadiness, perhaps needing surgical or drug interventions. But, in good health there are very real electrical pulses from the sinoatrial node, which is nature's pacemaker in the flesh, for the heart and housed in the right atrium chamber, that drive heart contractions. Those contractions are imbued with a rhythm (also called a pulse or heart rate) that a babe in utero is bathed in – how beautiful is that?! And which an infant feels and hears, cradled next to their mother's heart. With sustained parental feelings of love and appreciation, the infant's heart and breathing can entrain to the parent's heart rhythm. Our grown-up hearts are beating 100,000 times per day, adding up to 3 billion beats in a lifetime, and we hardly even notice. All of this enterprise has a purpose to keep us alive. It's a monumental job and the heart takes center-stage.

The potential for error in heart functioning, misuse and abuse, blood clots, blockages, shut-downs, electrical disturbances, chemical imbalances, damage, cardiac arrests and more is massive as in a massive heart attack that is almost bound to kill. Heart disease is our nation's number one cause of death. And, to handle that challenge, we have a myriad of offerings to heal the heart. In a sentence, the medic's expertise in surgeries and drugs, the energy worker's helping to restore your wellness, plus your own choices in lifestyle changes cover a lot of heart territory. But, feeling and being the love is the most important thing of all, my heart tells me, to make all treatments that we choose be the best that they can be.

The hardships of illness, infirmity and fear are what we are likely to confront on this earthly plane. We can decide that for own well-being of body, mind and spirit we can learn to overcome the challenges by whatever means suits us. It may or may not cure but we can heal. My cardiologist nephew tells all his patients three things, "Eat well. Exercise. Let Go." For addressing life style changes which could impact your health, that about covers it, as brief as you can get, for heart health. It certainly will heal. And it might even cure.

A doctor friend of mine told me a few months ago about a seeming miracle with a patient who was scheduled for heart surgery. A year earlier the cardiologist colleague of my friend had said that the woman had too much damage to her heart to risk any further surgery. She could come back in a year and decide how to proceed. So, her family went into crisis mode. They created a network of people, enough to know that someone or more was always 'in action' to pray for this woman to be healed. Their positive thoughts and imploring prayers to God, their higher power, for her heart to be well were sent in a steady stream heavenward – for one year!! At the end of the year she returned to her team of doctors for their tests and evaluations. No doctor in the hospital could believe it or explain it but everything was normal! They were all in awe of the woman's recovery and no one had any medical explanation for her now well-functioning heart. Can you and I venture a reason for her healed heart? Of course! She was healed by a steady stream of love, filling and fixing her being, repairing, balancing, fine tuning as with a musical instrument, bringing her whole system back into homeostasis and into the glow of love and health. That love came from above and all around the energy-filled universe that we humans are a part of and are filled with and it spread like a golden light to anyone with a heart open to love. That's a miracle.

A person's *broken heart* comes from disappointment, loss and grief. And, as seasoned humans, you must know, there are a lot of broken hearts out there. Someone has rejected and disappointed them, not met their expectations and left them bereft and alone. It's a very let-down load of sadness that takes over the psyche and won't let go. A broken heart is not just a metaphoric expression. It is physically bad for the heart if one keeps hanging on to hurts and grievances. As my heart doctor nephew said, "Let Go!" As in *Tashlich*, a ritual that Jews practice on the first day of Rosh Hashanah, to symbolically cast off their sins, throw all your emotional pain to the waters as you toss bread pieces in a lake or stream to flow away with your tears and never be seen or felt again. I'm not Jewish but I've done it once a couple of years ago, when a Jewish friend described it to me on the day of Rosh Hashanah and I ran to a brook a few blocks from my home before dusk turned to darkness and tossed my bread pieces into the water. The prophet Micah, in Micah 7:19, said after casting their sins into the depths of the sea, "He (G-d) will take us back in love." And I returned home with a lighter heart. Love seems to be part of everything.

I have heard people ask and have read this question in real life stories, "Do you know what heals the human heart?" And the answer is "Love!" And, guess what, this works for the metaphoric heart heavy with emotional pain as well as the heart in need of a cardiologist's skilled work to bring our physical heart back to normal function. We're not alone in knowing that love heals.

For as far back as recorded history informs us, the heart was considered the seat of thinking. The ancient Egyptians (around 1500 BC to 50 BC) said that the heart was where the soul resided with memory, emotions, personality and human wisdom. In their Book of the Dead, your heart had to be light as a feather, as weighed by the god Anubis, in order to enter the afterlife. Doing good deeds during your lifetime made for a light heart. Doesn't that fit well with our thinking, 3,500 years later? Doing good things, which, if your heart is in it, means you are a vessel of love and compassion. Your load is light which is good for any heart in my book.

Aristotle, born in 384 B.C., said intelligence, sensation and motion came from the heart. And that way of thinking carried for centuries until anatomists learned about circulation on vivisection from Realdo Columbo in the 1500s AD. Over decades and centuries since, we have learned more and more about the brain, the heart and other organs and their functions. And with that expanded knowledge, the focal point for consciousness became more the brain. But, not all thinkers gave up on the heart being the center of our thinking and feelings. Research has supported the hearts neuronal network's intelligence and the display of emotional content from our hearts. The physical is real. The metaphoric is beautiful. The heart is the heart and soul of our physical, mental, emotional and spiritual lives. All those parts of ourselves are interwoven and held together by our heartstrings. Physical and metaphoric, the chordae tendinae anchor our precious heart valves to our heart muscles, with the heart being called one big muscle. What a miracle pumping muscle it is and never to be seen, except by a heart surgeon. Tucked into our chest cavity and pulsing away like our lives depended on it and being our connecting place for all the aspects of ourselves that matter.

Try this. In your heart-smart heart, focus on your heart. Put all your thoughts, feelings and imaginings at the core of your being. Focus with your mind's eye on the beauty of the heart's function, its steadiness and its commitment to keeping your body alive and at a peak of health. Immerse yourself in the love because that's what hearts are made of and that be you. Say thank you to your heart and watch love fill all the spaces like a cup runneth over in Psalms 23:5. Let emotions well up because that is what hearts do and it touches our hearts. Just glory in the connection with all that is and for as long as you can sustain it. Breathe deeply and release. And slowly open your eyes to the world around you filled with love.

And the fields! Besides the neural network of the heart, brain and body, all delivering information both ways that we've already talked about, we have both the heart and brain communicating information via their electromagnetic fields that are projected out by both the brain and the heart in circular waves radiating outside our bodies. The field of the heart has been measured to be 60 times greater in amplitude than the field of the brain. Is that because the heart has more to say? The heart's magnetic component is 5000 times stronger that the brain's magnetic field. Does that show the urgency and importance of the heart to send a message to others? Magnetometers several feet away from the heart can detect the field. The heart's field seems to serve as a carrier wave for information shared with the entire body. So, we have pulsing and enfolding waves of energy radiating out from the heart and interacting with organs and throughout other parts of the body. Try feeling it with your hands or seeing it with your eyes. What does all this say?

The heart has capabilities that maybe only the ancient Egyptians and Aristotle would have imagined. They honored the heart as the center of being. We know today that the heart influences the brain in its perception, cognition and emotional processing. That's high level functioning and the heart has a part in it. The heart having stronger and greater fields than the fields of the brain makes for even more exchange of information within the body and with other humans as social beings and yes, with our animal friends. It's no wonder that we fall in love with those who touch our hearts. The energy fields are spreading the love.

So, I send kudos to the heart for sending and responding to the positive emotions of love and appreciation, bringing a smooth and coherent pattern to the heart's rhythmic activity. That brings positive changes to the electromagnetic field and it is radiated by the heart. It adds up to better emotional balance, mental clarity, and cognitive function. When you get to the core of it, love is at the heart of it all.

Dr. Shinichi Suzuki was the renowned Japanese musical educator and creative thinker who conceived and started a whole new school of teaching musical instruments. I have two grandsons who were taught at a very young age by teachers of the Suzuki Method. Dr. Suzuki famously said, "First foster the heart, then help the child acquire ability. This is indeed nature's proper way." What he meant by this is that the teacher is to first nurture the spirit of the person being taught. (Yes, their spirit!) Be sensitive to pupils who are in emotional pain for a myriad of possible reasons and show your support of that boy or girl's heavy-heart by caring, waiting and listening without judgement. Then you can pass on the knowledge of musical structure and form and of the skill and discipline of music.

It touches my heart to this day to think that the teacher's willingness to listen might transform any barriers and make room for musical progress. Being present, waiting, listening to their voice, without judging, showing compassion and caring are all part of what love is. Love reveals the whole package of emotional goodies in its all-encompassing energy. And then, with that support, the pupil can play their instrument with more confidence and joy. I've seen it. How about we apply that thinking to all our educational opportunities? What a great world this would be!

And, just to show the marvel of a teacher first giving space to love, to listen and to care, which nourishes the spirit, and then to teach the discipline and skill of music, with my grandsons, here's an update. We know that there can be many factors that affect a child's growth and development, but the Suzuki approach I've described, I think was an important influence in what my grandsons came to be. One went on to be a genius with nearly twenty spoken and written languages. And music is a language too! The other, a tech entrepreneur, is in his other time a gifted French hornist with orchestras and musical groups throughout the University area. His heritage is a grandmother – me, who loved and played the French horn with enough skill to compete in state level competitions and a father (my son-in-law) who was way more skilled than me on the horn. And, my grandson's accomplishments on the horn go beyond his father's. I think a heart and spirit filled with love started it all.

"Have an open heart," we hear from the new age gurus. In this heart of mine's view, an open heart is open to know and experience the world full of blemishes and harm and to have no fear. Your open heart is filled to overflowing with love. Receiving and giving of that love happens with ease. There is no withholding or tightness, nor saving it for another time. The spigot is open with an outpouring of love for the good of all at any time or place. That is grace, in case you haven't heard that word for a while! And what is grace? It is love without a reason or having to be, that surprises us with its beauty and touching of our hearts. Grace shows in affectionate acts that occur without explanation at any minute of the day. Grace is the love, unconditional and whole as the cosmic consciousness that is all connected as one, that we all would wish for and that our body, mind, emotions and spirit reap benefits from for a lifetime. It is part and parcel of the love force permeating the universe in which we are blessed to be integral with the Whole.

And here's an intriguing heart capability beyond what is 'normal' in our physical world. It's called intuitive perception. Some researchers have found the heart's energetic field gets information about a future event before the event happens and that the heart appears to receive this "intuitive" information before the brain. Not believable you say, but the suggestion is that the heart's energetic field may be linked to a more subtle field that contains information on objects and events remote in space or ahead in time. And I bring it up to open up our thinking on possible but unknown workings of the forces in the cosmos (remember physicists stretching our thinking by saying decades ago that 3 dimensions might not be the limit, it could be a dozen or more, which seemed impossible to us – and then we changed our minds?). This subtle energetic field of intuition is a system of potential energy that enfolds space and time (imagine the beauty of that!), and it is thought to be the basis for our consciousness of 'the whole,' which I spoke of early in the book. If there's truth to it, that adds even more intrigue to our heart's surprising capacities for knowing and feeling. I am bewitched with the thought that there is knowledge that we might have written on our hearts and that we have not yet uncovered.

I wonder and ask is it possible that love and appreciation generate coherence in the heart field not only to enhance health and well-being, which I believe it does, but also to make the energetic field more intuitively receptive? The heart and intuition seem to have gone hand-in-hand for centuries. "I knew it in my heart" and "In my heart of hearts." Or is it all best left to metaphor?

And then, dear ones, we have the good-ness that we all can be. Higher and higher up on our ladder of wellness and being is the wholeness of love. It is golden, for the ones who are aware, as in "She has a heart of gold." All weights have been cast off. Sadness and fear are overtaken by this strongest of heart throbs. Love informs every action and cancels out the hurtful times. It imbues the spirit. My heart is keeping right. And you don't need to be religious or believe in an ideology to have a compassionate heart, but if you do that serves you, too. The Dalai Lama says that "The essence of any religion is good heart." Make it your own. Just out of love, reach to be the best of yourself. And you'll know your heart is keeping right.

I've sung and played the hymn, 'If Your Heart Keeps Right' (lyrics and music written by Lizzie DeArmond and Bentley D. Ackley in 1912 - I want to give credit where credit is due and so continue to keep my heart right!), many dozens of times and my spirit sheds a tear or more of gladness every time.

If your heart keeps right, if your heart keeps right,
There's a song of gladness in the darkest night.
If your heart keeps right, if your heart keeps right,
Every cloud will wear a rainbow, if your heart keeps right.

Chapter 9

WHAT WE DO FOR WHAT AILS US

As an exercise in scanning the field and getting the picture, let's take an introductory look at some examples of what the medical and mostly alternative fields for health are offering and what the future might hold when it comes to treating disease and promoting health. And I will put those files that I've kept going for decades, to more use. If something important is out of date but good for the conversation I'll say it. But, most in-depth information and knowing is left up to the reader to search out.

There are other things besides describing diseases, to recognize about health. For centuries we have persons and groups and cultures that have opinions and philosophical views of health. They have their own understanding of what goes wrong and then what modalities can make us and keep us well.

Raymond Francis, a chemist, in *Never Be Sick Again* © 2002 says that all diseases are caused by two things: nutritional deficiency and toxicity. Some call it a revolutionary theory of health and disease. There is only one disease-- that of malfunctioning cells, only two causes of disease (deficiency and toxicity), and six pathways to health and disease-- nutrition, toxins, psychological, physical, genetic, and medical. So, I'm seeing that if one examines each of those descriptions, causes and pathways a person should be able to attribute whatever illness they are experiencing to those things. I don't know how it works in practice but it could be a useful way to understand better the 'what and why' of getting sick. And I would add LOVE to the mix.

And here's a twist on our exploring a few of the many 100s of diseases we see today. Qi Gong says in *HEAL YOURSELF with Qi Gong* © 2009, pg.43, by Sifu George Picard, that there is only ONE disease regardless of how many labels we use. Every disease has a starting point and it is in the realm of energy or Qi. It begins with the cell. Each cell strives to maintain homeostasis and is a micro-universe unto itself. If the cell is deficient in Qi it cannot function properly and will break down. If the cell is toxic from the chemicals in our food and the food itself is poor (bad food Qi), the cell cannot function as it should. Now the labels of disease come out and the illness process begins. With the practice of Qi Gong, the Qi impacts all systems from the cell on up which helps the cells to function at a higher level, and healing can take hold. All systems are … constantly working to balance the system. By my thinking, Qi is the equivalent of love energy. If it is low, disease starts. When love energy fills our cells and our entire being, our system becomes balanced and healing pervades the whole body organism.

In *Reinventing the Body, Resurrecting the Soul* © 2009, Deepak Chopra wrote about an energy healer friend who saw a dinner guest's hand tremble when he reached for something. He was in his late thirties and said he had Parkinson's disease (average age of onset is 60). The energy healer invited the man to a weekend training workshop in Qigong. This Chinese healing directs qui, the basic life-force of the body. Its natural flow can get imbalanced. The teacher had a new idea of unraveling the trauma by healing tiny mistakes in the qi, one at a time, like tiny links in a chain. The guest's tremors decreased dramatically while at the course, but it's not known what happened afterward. Something was working and we don't know for how long. But there is intrigue in the idea of correcting mistakes in the qi with a pattern of disciplined movements. Qi is a field, like a magnetic field and he envisioned the energy going down the spine, the main pathway of energy in Qigong. And, as I said a paragraph ago, in my mind's eye, that is love energy working its wonders.

For 40,000 years Native American medicine has been healing humans of their ills. The wisdom of a wide array of Indians throughout our country and the world has been passed down orally for centuries. We are the oh-so-fortunate recipients of their wisdom that might have been lost forever, but was at least partly recovered. Their understanding was and is that we are part of nature and health is a matter of balance. They have lived by honoring and keeping in harmony our interrelationships with all living things. Many aspects of this cannot be seen by the eye or by modern technology, but are experienced directly and intuitively. The integration of our inner life forces and nature's forces makes for balance and health. How this healing is put into practice has been kept, seemingly intentionally, secret among the tribes until recently we see it slowly being revealed by brave tribal members before the knowledge is totally lost. The spirit is a prominent aspect of living and cures and if there are human imbalances, then their tribal spiritual interventions might take place. Ceremonies led by respected elders (is that respect missing in our own culture and to our detriment?) give honor to the world of spirits. I think the group dynamics of this is a manifest of belonging. Everyone is cared for and supported with their tribe and share the same desires to make well what is out of sorts. This is pure love, as I see it, in its highest form to create balance and wellness. And it's been practiced for many thousands of years!

And here's a health view from decades ago. As a young girl, if I had a fever, my mother, knowing by putting her hand on my forehead and seeing my malaise, put me to bed for rest and quiet for days. The body needs all its energy for healing, not activity. She didn't see the fever as a bad thing but as something the body needed to do to deal with germs, viruses and unknown invaders. There was good reason, as she saw it, that the body was 'acting up' to overcome, get rid of or silence whatever 'imbalance agent' wanted to take over your body function and you needed to 'sweat it out.' But, you didn't want the heat to get too hot, so a cold cloth on the forehead made me a little more comfortable. If it was a 'chest cold' she put Vicks Vapor Rub under my nose and on my chest and covered it with a flannel cloth to 'cure' and help my body overcome the infection. There were no antibiotics then, so my body's immune system was put to the task and was even better able to deal with another assault to my health if it came along. It's nice to be immune to something that does not serve you well and it is good to brush off all ills and negativity.

All seven of us kids survived very nicely into adulthood. Sarah, my mother, would say in a nutshell, let nature take its course, support the body healing itself, and give yourself plenty of rest. And, most importantly, give and receive love and prayers from God. She herself was a Biblical 'cup runneth over' love vessel. Love was and is freely and intensely given while the body is searching and working to reach its own balance for health. I see a lot of wisdom in her practices. We don't take time today to recover from illness and instead, push ahead, with the help of drugs to dampen symptoms and at the same time, repress our body's own immunity, to get back to activity. In a long ago era, there was no rush to heal. We can learn from the past, as smart as we may be in this modern era. And I would wish that the compassion of love would fill everyone who has health challenges to face and healing and recovery to generate.

Sarah believed in miracles and the Bible she read every day is filled with miracles that Jesus made happen by a touch of his hand or with a word. In Matthew chapters 8 and 9, Jesus went up into a mountain, gathering his disciples along the way, teaching and blessing them, and returned to see multitudes. He touched a woman's hand and healed her of a fever. He went on to cast out the spirits of people, possessed by devils, with his word. He told a man, sick in bed with a palsy, "Son, be of good cheer; thy sins be forgiven thee. Arise, take up thy bed, and go unto thine house." And he arose and departed to his house. And Jesus beheld a woman diseased for 12 years and called dead, who touched his garment, saying she would be whole. Jesus said, "Daughter, be of good comfort; thy faith hath made thee whole." And the woman was made whole from that hour. He touched two blind men's eyes and they could see. Seeing the multitudes, he was "moved with compassion" for them. He went about the cities and villages teaching and healing every sickness and every disease among the people. This healer of the masses was the exemplar of caring, compassion and mercy – mercy, the beautiful and underused word for forgiveness. All virtues add up to Love Heals. Maybe it's no wonder that miracles happen.

Other healing powers and potions from the past that are given new life today are taking sage for memory lapses, pressing painful spots of strain and stress on the body for a couple of minutes as in acupressure. Chew or sip ginger in tea for nausea. Swish oil of cloves in your mouth for a painful tooth. Drink unsweetened (sugar feeds an infection) cranberry juice for a urinary tract infection. Take my dad's honey from his many dozens of bee hives in the mid-1900s and use as a salve for wounds and mix with lemon juice to swish and swallow for a sore throat. Chew fennel seeds, as seen at checkout in Indian restaurants, to prevent belching and gas. Drink black cherry juice for inflammation of arthritis. Use aloe vera directly on burns. All summarized in a nutshell – home to a rich source of protein.

Do you want to live longer? Do these five things: no smoking, drink moderately, keep a healthy weight, exercise regularly and eat well. Studies show in a sampling of well over 100,000 that men and women who practice these five things live a dozen years more than the rest of the population.

And would you like a 'lift' when you're in turmoil with hurts and feeling down, mostly from human encounters, rejection or lack of connections with other humans, close or distant? Feel the pain, calm your thoughts, find the love, and if you cannot quite make it to the glorious distant rise on the mountain or you just want to stay 'human' a little longer (!) just ACCEPT where you're at and what is there. There's painful stuff you've tried many ways to deal with, with some or no good resolution, and you're tired of trying, good for you. Just let go of the trying, give yourself a rest and smile for one thing that is happening in your life or see one thing that you appreciate in the person you love. Put to rest the rest. If the humanity you are experiencing is discordant and too much to bear, send them love. It is the best fixer-upper. Love alone could add years to your life and give space to more happiness – and even more love. What a gift for everyone!

Our own 'Western world' system of finding what went wrong in our bodies and how we can 'right' it is dominated by science and technology. Diagnostic tests give data of solid numbers that can likely put you in categories that have their own workable solutions, as it is with a person having swollen joints and low-grade fever and showing a positive factor on an RA or rheumatoid arthritis test. The protocol says to use steroids and anti-inflammatory agents to reduce the pain, inflammation and RA activity. This will probably be a lifetime management project and many people with RA do muster up what it takes to carry on their lives and fulfill their desires. But, in addition to or instead of, if a person refuses the drugs or if the protocol is severely injurious to the person, there may be other modalities to pursue if we search and find some to our liking and which may help us cope better or ease the symptoms or even bring us back to a normal balance and cure - it does happen!

Remembering that we are talking about all areas of health including physical, mental, emotional and spiritual health, here are some complementary modalities practiced in our modern age, often from the long-ago past, beyond what pharmaceuticals and traditional medical treatments prescribe today, that might work for whatever ails you and that you are probably familiar with and may be doing already in your life's journey. And know that practitioners of modern medicine today are far more welcoming of alternative, lesser known treatments for all your ills than ever in the past. I think they are glad to expand their options of referral and to give you some choices in treatments that might well put you on the road to better health – for all four bodies that make up who you are.

So, in alphabetical order, I'll name some of the 100s of healing offerings out there, many of which I've experienced, just to provoke your thinking and perhaps impact any or all of your emotional, physical, mental and spiritual bodies of health. Then you can carry on a search of your own for what might work for you, what you need to be cautious about, what risks if any there are for you, costs you can manage and what you feel intuitively could make a difference for your health. Feeling good about your pursuit is a significant benefit for results that you might hope for.

The list starts with acupuncture. Then we have Alexander technique, aqua therapy, aromatherapy, art, astrology, Ayurvedic medicine, Bach flower therapy, chelation therapy, chromotherapy (using colors to adjust body vibrations to frequencies that result in health and harmony), colloidal silver therapy, colon hydrotherapy, craniosacral therapy and crystal healing,

And, catch your breath, here's more: cupping, dance therapy, dietary supplements, diet, distant healing, dowsing, ear candling, electromagnetic field therapy, faith healing, fasting, Feldenkrais method, Feng shui, flower essence therapy, guided imagery, hair analysis, herbal medicine, homeopathy, horticultural therapy, hydrotherapy, hypnosis and iridology.

And then laughter therapy, light therapy, massage of many kinds, medical intuition, meditation of all sorts, music therapy (included in sound therapy), numerology, osteopathic medicine, Pranic healing, and prayer (mainstream for many), psychic surgery (as with John of God in Brazil), Qi Gong, rebirthing, reflexology, reiki, Rolfing, and sound therapy (music, tones, binaural beats, alpha waves, birds singing, isochronic pulses). I have a very health-minded and practiced friend in Berkeley who 15 years ago, told me about a friend of hers who had prostate cancer. He did music therapy and he was cured, she said with certainty. I don't know his status today.

And to finish up my list are spiritual healing, Tai chi, therapeutic horseback riding, therapeutic touch, visualization, and yoga coming in many types.

Since I have been treated with many of these complementary therapies, I can say that they are a pleasure to experience as well as a healing of the highest order. I feel embraced as well as supple with the attention given me in Thai massage and reiki. My sense of smell is stimulated for the good in my walks in nature and in aromatherapy as I imagine all the good things that it does. I take pleasure in feeling and hearing the tones vibrating my auditory nerve branches in my own sound therapy of music, recorded and live, with my favored piano, viola and horn and a wide range of tones from singing bells and bowls and, most touching to my spirit, the ringing vibrations coming from the small Tibetan brass bowl and wooden mallet that is a gift from my California daughter, bless her highly vibrating heart of goodness.

Most sickness and disease is the result of physical, mental, emotional or spiritual energy that's out of balance. The clear, pure energy that flows through a healer's hands brings the energy of the recipient back into balance and into harmony, thus helping to restore them back to health. Many healers, including Anthony William, author and medical medium, have said that compassion is the most important element in healing. A healer's caring and giving love and attention to help alleviate someone's pain and suffering is work of the highest order. The energy of love connection vibrates within us and surrounding us.

And this is what all the healing modalities are. The secret is out. As if I've been keeping it under wraps and saving it for the end! The practitioners are all ENERGY healers. It's all about energy. And the all-encompassing energy can only be LOVE. There is no higher vibration in the cosmos! There is no greater ONENESS of source.

Energy is coming from a higher more expansive space and place. This energy is all-encompassing and is filling the universe. Love fills and flows through a healer's hands and heart. The vibrating love fills your hurting parts and entire being. It puts your worries to rest. It warms your heart to accept and expect a glow of health. That goes for any healing modality you pick. It is all energy vibrations. And I say, indubitably and unapologetically, the energy is overwhelmingly, all inclusively, encompassing LOVE. You are cradled in an outpouring of love. Any negativity, harm, pain, illness is done away with and overcome by the higher forces of love. Think it! Believe it! Feel it! Let the cascade of loving vibrations fill you up to the brim. This is energy medicine of the highest order.

There is immense pleasure in the gift of someone working hands-on for your needy parts. But, you don't have to have an energy healer working on you to feel the vibrating energy of love. Alone in my living space, yoga fills my being with gliding movement every day. There is joy in laughter therapy -- I do it alone and deliberately to shake my body and smile. I know I am doing good things for my health and longevity when I have carefully chosen vital food throughout almost all the decades of my life. My light therapy machine is stimulating my eyes with hopefully a good dose of regeneration for aging parts. Years ago, homeopathy led me on a path of overcoming joint problems and returning to full action and movement. And the list goes on. It's all to the good of encouraging the flow of love throughout all my bodies.

I think all these healing treatments are cherished by the physical body, as well as the mental, emotional and spiritual aspects of ourselves and are a big support to get us back on track with health. They all say love yourself. You're worth it. Be kind to yourself by treating yourself to a massage. We love you and give you the best of what the universe channels through our healers. It all crystalizes to the multi-faceted jewel of love.

Face it! We all want to be loved. Appreciated. Heard. Noticed. We want and need confirmation of who we are. We look for validation of ourselves. But, on this earthly plane and higher as our love consciousness rises, know that there is no need to receive. And I emphasize the word 'need.' We're not impoverished or deprived. Just 'let go' and make room for the love. Love comes as a gift if we open our hearts to receive it. With full hearts, we, in turn, give effortlessly from that store of love. Watch for sublime things to happen for the vibrant health of all!

The body is designed to heal itself. Hippocrates said it and it is still widely believed today. My dad said it too and guided his own health with that belief and with the axiom, mind over matter. With mind over matter, you help the body to heal its own self. Let's do everything possible to set the stage for health and healing in our physical form and nature will pick up on the clue to heal its' very own self. Love is the guide.

As with my marine scientist friend, resentment vanished and love remains, healing all her wounds. Her forgiveness and understanding made room for love to thrive.

From your ever-lovin' author, in any difficult situation that you might be inclined to give in to feeling pain and sadness, if you understand and forgive in your heart, then love takes over. Love is the tip, the pointer, the key, the tip-off to support our bodies, minds, emotions and spirits to become well and radiate good health and love from all to all.

And, it bears repeating what I wrote in BIG Balance. "You could sum this up for all health challenges by seeing and saying that you have a clear INTENTION to be well AND you know that it is POSSIBLE to be in full, vibrant health."

Lynn Cox, record setting, open-water swimmer in intense cold, a supreme athlete and author of *Swimming in the Sink* © 2016, was searching for a 'mind shift' – a new way of thinking that would help her escape the intense pain of her hand near frozen is a research project of endurance. Just as Dr. Roger Bannister, British runner and neurologist who broke the world record in 1954 by running a mile in less than four minutes achieved that mind shift. What was thought to be impossible became possible. Shortly after his success, other runners ran the mile in under four minutes. The mind set had changed! And it did for Lynn as well as they completed the research project with extraordinary results.

Give yourself a mind shift. Imagine clearly your INTENTION and believe that all things are POSSIBLE. As Jesus said to the father of a child needing healing in Mark 9:23 KJV: If thou canst believe, all things are possible to him that believeth.

My dad would applaud.

Chapter 10

You Can Say I Love You

In the middle of my Thai massage today on Friday, my therapist was moving the joints of my feet with gentle pushes as I shared with her a recent incident with someone where my feelings were hurt. I admitted to my therapist that it was an ego-centric thing that I had felt hurt and that I had worked quickly at the time to turn it around and get back on an upward path, knowing that whatever was going on with someone else, emotionally close to me or distant, didn't have to affect me badly. I am the one to decide how I feel. Others have their own path, with their own challenges and their own ways of living and responding to life, as do I. There is no need for hurt at all! And my Thai therapist looked up gently at me and said, "I love you."

Now, this touches my heart. She heard and understood my story of emotional pain and my quick release from that pain and her comment was love.

You, dear persons, who are sharing the planet! Don't you wish the world could work that way all the time?

It can! Yes, it can! Now, let's take it further and say and believe that love has the power to heal not just everyone but the planet, too. After all, I daringly said early on in this book that love-infused conscious awareness created the whole cosmos! That is love. And that's no small thing. Love creates and is the source of creation. And it can heal one soul and tree at a time. Anyone can be appreciated for their love of the planet, no matter what their politics of party or point of view for what to do.

Inclusion, not exclusion, keeps love front and center. If you make pure water or anything else your cause, whatever your party affiliation or not, should not matter. Share your love, don't withhold it. We're all together in trying to figure it all out and anyone can (pardon the pun) tap into the conscious oneness for a possible creative solution for the health of all persons' all four bodies and the surroundings we dwell in as well.

A siege on one group over another could mean that the good work to bring love and healing to all is made tougher. Open hearts make for health-ful starts. Keeping an open, inclusionary way of being could foster entrepreneurs to create solutions for our health in ways you might not imagine. These creative thinkers, by nature, working in the free marketplace rather than a government controlled bureaucracy, might well come up with less polluting means to power our cars and engines, or to neutralize, transform and rid the earth of chemicals and radiation that can kill us. Or help find a simple, cost-free way to distill water from air – of which several devices have already been invented and won awards. This could be a major breakthrough in providing water to keep us cool on those days when it's not. Where there is cooperation and good will a loving environment grows and makes for a healthful place for creative thinking that could lead to inventions that help us as earthlings and make better the earth home we live in.

And there's more cooling to do. From the MIT News Office on November 28, 2018 comes a new way to provide cooling without power. MIT researchers created a passive system using inexpensive materials with no need for fossil fuel-generated power to supplement other cooling systems for food and medication preservation in off-grid locations on hot summer days. A metal strip above the device blocks the sun's direct rays, like an umbrella, that allows heat emission at mid-infrared light range to pass through the atmosphere, rising through the greenhouse gases and then radiate into cold outer space.

Science research funding for a plethora of things to benefit both people and the environment, coming from government allotments as well as private enterprise grants, makes for a healthy, cooperative mix found in academic settings and research facilities across the country. It's not far afield to go from a loving, all inclusionary environment to freewheeling ideas and leapfrogging progress on many scientific fronts. Giving researchers and entrepreneurs a freer environmental setting of expressing love for ALL opens the door, as I quoted in an earlier chapter, Hal David's words to Burt Bacharach's music, "What the world needs now is love, sweet love, No not just for some but for everyone." That's huge and the repercussions are timeless and beyond the horizon. And it starts with one voice saying "I love you."

Saying "I love you," brings out, in the open, all our love. As you might innocently say in a children's book, "I love you," to the illustration of a gorgeous panorama of nature's snow-covered mountains and green spruce ascending the heights. Thank you for sharing your beauty. We'll do what we can to keep you healthy and growing. And our love is the most important thing. It motivates us to treat you well and it creates and fertilizes all life and cures us, too. Our knowing and flowing says that all life is love. You feel it and share it and say it, "I love you!"

When you see or know of someone who is hurting in their physical frame or in their feelings as well as their thoughts, say, "I love you."

Certainly to yourself, but out loud too, if it seems right to do. The benefits to you and others can be immense. Don't you want to make a difference while you're fortunate enough to have a life on this physical plane that is our home in the skies? Lucky us! Share the love. Say "I love you!" And when you are the 'someone' hurting keep your love cistern full.

Many people don't easily say, "I love you." But, there are many who do and good for you! For the others, the quiet ones, even very close to us, there seems to be an inhibition and reluctance to mouth those words. In writing, as in a personal letter, we'll sometimes see a sign-off of 'love' but way less often is "I love you" written to a friend or family. Try saying and writing, "I love you!" You might like it! And others might, too. We can start a movement! And change the world – one soul at a time.

Innocent children are sometimes our best teachers. If you grew up in a home, disturbing to your healthy emotional growth and not being attended to in your physical growth or needs of mind, you're in an extra challenging place on your path of living a life. Some can't make their way out of the depressive milieu and don't survive. Others in a miraculous turn seem to 'know' what could be and rise above their surroundings to embrace love and health. They found a way to connect with that big love source and give love away to any one open to receiving it. It is amazing to see; it boggles the mind, touches the heart and stirs the emotions with tears of love. Some have even managed when grown up and on their own, to see their parents and others, who enabled their childhood abuse and neglect, with compassion and to say the emotionally freeing phrase, "I love you."

"There is an ocean of love behind all of this fear and pain," says Michael A. Singer, author of *The Untethered Soul*. "That force will sustain you by feeding your heart from deep within. … Now peace and love will run your life." How true that is – and wonderful!

"I love you so much!" my college granddaughter in the Northwest has texted me and told me in person when we write or talk. And another college granddaughter, on the East Coast, has said or written me many times in signing off, "I love you, Grandma." As does my college grandson, in the Midwest, saying "I love you, too." You don't 'need' anything with that kind of love. They are practiced in it and what a gift it is to give and to receive. And it unites us from shore to shore, the full breadth of our country, through all parts of the good old USA.

And how to encourage that love exchange? Mother Teresa said, "Let us always meet each other with a smile, for a smile is the beginning of love." Right on! I smile at almost everyone I meet throughout my day and it just turns on the love. And kind words help, as we read in Proverbs 16:24 KJV, "Pleasant words are as an honeycomb, sweet to the soul, and health to the bones."

It's a beauteous and bewitching journey we are on. The twists and turns reveal mysteries uncovered for our searching minds. The climbs and descents tax our stamina and prowess. The curves give us opportunities to challenge and recover our balance. There are lessons to be learned and teachings of our own to pass on. And there is love covering it all, as a journalist covers the news. For your own sake and for all other sets of ears, say it again and one more time. "I love you," to the Universe, created out of love, and to anyone else who's listening.

Chapter 11

SPIRIT

I just took my usual, early three mile walk, this time in the dark. Five-thirty a.m. on October 4, 2018, means that the sun does not rise until 7:11. Remember when all quick shops with snacks, food and gas were called 'Seven Eleven?' Is there meaning and a reason for this coincidental snap to the past? Perhaps, it brought to my attention that few things in life are a quick fix. Take it slow and easy in pondering the answers to what do I do with feeling distressed with people's behavior or reminding me to keep looking for messages above in the skies or below on terra firma. I'll take that as a lesson of the day.

We have had weeks of Hurricane Florence and then Hurricane Michael in North Carolina, with non-ending wetness and gray skies. I'm a lover of the stars – call me star-struck (with love!), but they have been hidden for a long time with the clouds of watery mist filling the atmosphere. I stepped out onto the road with my flashlight and I looked up.

"Orion, my hunter in Greek mythology, you're back!" All seven - God's Biblical number, as it is mine, of your major stars are shining brightly! Betelgeuse (with my name inside minus the 'h'), the second brightest star in Orion, defines the right shoulder of the hunter. Betelgeuse is a red giant and looking red with its quickly expending energy and in near death throws to a spectacular supernova explosion in a hundred or a million years, no one knows, down the proverbial cosmic pike. It shines as the ninth brightest star in the night sky. Rigel, Orion's brightest star and usually seventh brightest in the sky, shapes the hunter's left knee. Rigel is a young blue giant or supergiant, as are all the other stars in Orion, except for Betelgeuse. As you can tell, I've had a special fondness for the constellation Orion and for these two brightest stars for many decades. They are a standout for me for connecting to the cosmos.

Orion! You are the hunter, just as I am hunting for the cause of everything and looking for answers to the other big questions of our existence! From my toddler days of huge curiosity and onward, my radiating passion is to think on what it's all about.

But the moon is shining too. There's a sliver of a waning crescent moon, visible just before sunrise and casting a little light on the macadam road, lucky for me, an early riser, as others have to set their alarms to catch this moon phase before dawn, when the moon slips down the horizon. The light of day will soon be taking over the visible sky, with the stars all hidden from view.

The light of coming dawn will illuminate the earth but at the same time, block from our view the stars, while the moon has set with the encroaching light. That's something to bear in mind when we are 'enlightened.' Don't forget the important things that might be obscured by an epiphany. Even though it sounds like an oxymoron! And there might be deeper meaning not obvious in the vision that we have to 'look' for to get the full scope. Such as a medium receiving multiple meaning messages, as Mark Anthony, medium and author of *Evidence of Eternity,* has pointed out with his stories. And, as in the military radioing secret encrypted messages piggy-backed on other more innocent messages to be alert for, there's more to it than meets the eye.

From this I'm reminded to keep my own light shining. That being my spirit! Especially in dark places where it could be a life-saver. It's the part of me that seems, in my both sensitive and logical self, to be part of a bigger source. Full of goodness and love to radiate out into the world. There are many of us individual humans with different wants, needs and behaviors, working to appreciate and learning to understand every other one in our lives, and longing for peace while feeling the bumps on the road and the hurtful impacts of our limited perceptions. Whatever the travails, we are all different notions of more, the more in totality being ONE. There is really no separation among us when we realize this Wholeness. So, instead of focusing on self as human, let's make the stretch, reach across the limits of being human to the 'stars,' the enlightenment, that can light up the spirit. And that is love. Your spirit body bridges your human aspect to the ONE that encompasses all things and beings. When you do that, good things happen.

With love, there is no separation. When you think and act apart from your spirit's inspiration, fear and other emotions that sap and zap your goodness take hold and you're likely to live your life with anxiety and guilt. Keep your spirit alive and well and in your awareness. There's no better elixir for your wellbeing. That connection with the whole is where you find love. Watch for it to happen.

This visible crescent of a moon shining in the dark, that I'm looking at, is a good time to see the features of the Moon's surface. Along the edge where the lit portion meets the dark side, the mountains and craters cast long shadows making them easier to observe with binoculars (mine are in my car but other times I've used them for a more detailed view of the heavenly bodies). And I make a mental note to see everyone through rose-colored glasses, do it consciously for a day and the world will be a better place to dwell in.

Seeing all this in the dark, I feel my own emotions and mental workings coming to life. Elation fills me with the astronomical magnificence overhead, along with hope for people-kind. Caring (for real!) is in my heart for the cosmos. Feeling thankful (that's a most health activating, sweet emotion of all, I do believe!) for all of creation that I can realize, and for love which encompasses all the good feelings we are capable of. There are no painful emotions to burden me. My thoughts of mind embrace the astronomical delights I am seeing with my physical eyes. All four bodies are in good health.

What is it that is moving me so? The grandness of it all for one thing. And the mystery. There are so many unanswered questions – what, why and wherefore, as my dad said time and time again. I can see the material reality of other sun-lights beside our own sun, filling the skies. By the laws of probability, at least some of the estimated 40 billion habitable zone, earth-sized planets around these Sun-like stars and red dwarf stars in the Milky Way galaxy must foster life in some form. There might also be others in other galaxies that are like us, or a variation or who exist as a lower or a higher form. It challenges our consciousness to take it all in.

It's easy to feel insignificant and small if we stay with our ego and earthly things. But I am struck with the realm I see high in the sky and then beyond to what I do not see.

Taking in the incredible heavenly display, feeling the grandeur of it all indubitably makes me think there has to be way more to it than just our finite human bodies. Our humanness can seem limited, inadequate and disappointing at times. But, let's look beyond the limitations, and uncover reasons and forces beyond our knowing. And that is where the spirit comes in. The spirit I feel, as part of my being, takes form as an unseen entity and always seems to rise above the fray of daily happenings in our material world. If there is health in spirit I have it. The realm of the spirit is of no time and no space. It goes beyond the physical and can be counted on to inspire all my mental faculties, emotional expressions and the well-being of this physical frame.

There is something in us that aspires to be good, to be a better person, to do good deeds, to be kind and loving. That part of ourselves is SPIRIT. Spirit is my urge and inspiration to rise above the fray with love-filled intention. If there is any lowering of spirit, I think it comes in the form of forgetting we have it. But, spirit is still there and I think, sharing a field with other spirits to inspire and embolden for the good of all.

Rumi, our poet of note as the most popular poet in the U.S., measured by the millions of books sold, said "Let music lessen our deafness to spirit. Play and let play." Music, reaching to the forces of a higher realm, can bring us all to awareness and attentiveness to our higher selves. Joy and fun vibrate at that high level and blend right in with the Spirit of Love. So, make music or listen to it to feed and grow the soul! From *Snow White and the Seven Dwarfs* (for fun!) comes Larry Morey and Frank Churchill's "Everything is in tune and its spring, And life flows along – With a Smile and a Song."

A part of me and my spirit is unrestrained reverence. It comes naturally, like it was always there, imbedded in a part of us all. I feel awe with the beauty and seeming magic of life. Awestruck is a lot like being star struck, I'm glad to say. It is our spirit that seems to tether between realms of material matter and a higher place. Our higher being is what it is.

Religions show this reverence and most call it honoring God with different names. The pantheist and the American Indian both honor and respect nature. The Shinto honor their ancestors with rituals to connect to their ancient past. The Buddhist gives honor to the Awakened One called the Buddha. I think all of us who aspire to be in that higher place are awakened ones. We've woken up to a wider world of love. This inspiriting has to be good for everyone's health! Being reverential brings out a good aspect of ourselves and reveals the never wavering goodness and well-being of spirit. All religions and groupings of reverence see what is present in their reverent practice with the eyes of their spirit or soul.

Hermann Hesse, a Nobel Prize winner, wrote 'Stages' at the beginning of his novel, *Magister Ludi*, published in 1943. "The Cosmic Spirit seeks not to restrain us But lifts us stage by stage to wider spaces."

That fits perfectly with the concept I'm describing. The Cosmic Spirit is the Oneness we tap into when we raise our spirits to a higher place with wider spaces. It bridges our being human with the whole. We are part of that whole of oneness of love's creation.

I felt that oneness in the late fall of 2018 on Topsail Island for two weeks with my children, their spouses and my grandchildren. I'd been finding a collection of shells in the shape of a heart on my beach walks. One day I asked Carl, my long-deceased husband, if he would lead me to a heart shaped shell. Within moments I found a beautiful one, the size of a big toe print in the sand, and I thanked him. There was spirit there of Carl, I felt in my head, in the air, and the beyond that he must be part of, with all the intimate experiences he and I have shared in spirit. I see him as part of the omniscient energy pervading the cosmos that came down to one heart shell with love. One of my granddaughters offered and put on fixings and with a 22" sterling silver chain it goes over my head and around my neck. I am one with Carl and the Spirit world and the heart shell is resting in steady, direct connection to my pulsing heart. Thank you, precious granddaughter and my dearest Carl. We are all one.

To broaden your soul experience, do this and it may be the best of all that presents for you and me. Walk or sit in nature – and that can be any-way, anywhere, anytime, including the beach! Spend as many moments as you can taking in the mysteries and beauty of what springs from the earth: plants, animals and landscapes. This is nourishment for the spirit.

My dear friend, Paul, who recently retired from a busy career, wrote me from England a while ago, telling me he was taking on a monastic way of life. He wrote, "Nature? No need to go anywhere.....trees, bushes, flowers, sky, sun, moon, dark, light, sunrise, sunset are right in front of us or above us always and everywhere. And for a full nature paradise a local park or beauty spot. I am blessed, the park is 100 yards away. The stillness and peace and flexibility, strength and rootedness of trees, the beauty and yearly cycle/transience of flowers, the 4 seasons, Spring - birth, Summer - bloom, Autumn - letting go, Winter - death, a never-ending cycle of rebirth and death, and we too are part of nature.

Who needs a cave to meditate or contemplate in? The inner life will produce mountains and valleys and deserts."

Who can deny the spiritual nature of things that my friend is speaking so eloquently about? We're all invited to spend as much time as we can in life's abundance, looking out a window at the falling leaves letting go or stepping outside to breath in the fragrance of the peonies in bloom in May, or traveling the globe and seeing Sirius, the brightest star in the sky, overhead on the desert sands in Egypt to nourish our spirit. Sirius appears at summer solstice, June 20-22, seventy days after it disappeared and also the standard period of mourning for ancient Egyptians. Just as Osiris, God of the afterlife was slain and mourned by his wife Isis for seventy days. The flooding of the Nile, in mythology, was caused by Isis's tears. Sirius was connected to Osiris's pain and Isis's faith. That brightest star held hope for the future and showed compassion for others, even our enemies, as an eternal source of navigation in life. Sirius's compassion is love and, even in the heavens above, love shines brighter than any other star.

Spirit is infused with love. The higher we raise our spirits the more love and light we manifest. What can be better for our health than pure love dwelling in our spirit and reaching every body cell, filling our emotional cistern and transforming our thoughts of mind? And then that love and spirit merge with all of creation.

Our 'all of creation' includes the animals. In the KJV Bible and the first chapter of the book of Genesis, God created animals and then man in our image and after our likeness, both on the same 6th day! We share a likeness including a growing awareness of spirit in our animal companions. Close up and around the clock living with an animal companion, most commonly a dog or cat has brought many testimonials to the existence of a soul or spirit of an animal. We've all heard them and maybe experienced them ourselves with a dog, cat, gerbil or parrot of one's own. Soulful eyes, steady looking with passion, connection and concern, tail wagging with its understanding that you have good intentions, lying down next to you and staying with you when you're sick, listening to every word and keeping their eyes connected with yours when you are unburdening your soul of the sad or disturbing intimacies of your life. Connection and comforting are there without any demands. Call that new or old true friend a soul dog in your life, a friend of your soul or spirit and a meeting of the minds and spirits. They enter your heart. Beyond the physical workings, there is something there that speaks of a higher awareness. I doubt anyone with an animal friend would think otherwise.

At a higher level of my spirit, with goodness filling my being, I'm bound to be in better health all around, inside and out. My physical self is in peak health. My psyche feels more at peace. The feel good emotions that one emits enhance our being and others' too which in turn is flourishing for our own living. A spirit-filled mind is a fertile ground for conceptualizing and imaginative brain action. Love rises above it like a mist to embrace us all.

The stars brought us together, from Orion to Sirius to our own planetary sun, moving steadily in a slow arc across the skies. Love is everywhere. It is on our earthly plane and in our hearts. Love is in the stars, because they came into being with the love force of consciousness. The total stellar population in the observable Universe is estimated to be seventy billion trillion or 7×10^{22}! No matter how many and how large and how distant the stars in the cosmos, love's vibrations fill the visible heavens and the worlds beyond. Our physical, mental, emotional and spiritual essence and the love that imbues the whole are one and the same. The love you seek is already here, is already you, and has always been so. The love we long for is ALL that is.